YOGA

has

to offer

What Yoga has to offer

Further lectures on the Yoga of Self-Knowledge

by Marjorie Waterhouse

SHANTI SADAN
LONDON

First published in 1996 by Shanti Sadan

29 Chepstow Villas
London W11 3DR

ISBN 0-85424-046-2

Printed and Bound by JB Offset Printers
Marks Tey, Colchester, Essex, Great Britain

CONTENTS

FOREWORD

Authority, based on personal experience, together with a warm humanity, mark the writings and lectures of Marjorie Waterhouse. This fusion of the sublime and the homely accounts for the popularity of her two books, *Training the Mind through Yoga* and *The Power Behind the Mind*, and has stimulated the demand for a further volume of her remaining unpublished lectures under the title *What Yoga Has to Offer*.

Marjorie Waterhouse often compared the spiritual path of Yoga to the ascent of a high mountain — the mountain of the mind. And she regarded every man and woman as potential mountaineers — that is, masters of their minds and emotions, and enjoyers of the spiritual wisdom of mankind.

It was a considered analogy, and she herself knew the mountain as if it rested on the palm of her hand: the roads to the base camp, the foothills, with their meandering paths and thickets; the windy and invigorating uplands; and finally the summit, where all preceding stages are seen in a new and comprehensive perspective. There was no more competent mountain guide than she herself to lead the would-be climbers, and monitor and aid their progress through the various phases of the ascent.

Having met her teacher, Hari Prasad Shastri, in 1931, she soon became one of the main supporters of his work in England. When he died in 1956, it was she who became Warden of Shanti Sadan, and who ensured the continued propagation and practice of the teachings of Adhyatma Yoga in accordance with the ancient tradition.

She herself always disclaimed any eminence as a teacher. One of her lectures begins, disarmingly:

> Friends! Before we begin our talks here, we always make our position as speakers clear to our audiences. We are all pupils here, not teachers, but *we have had a great Teacher* — Hari Prasad Shastri — and he was insistent on the fact that the Truth he gave us should be made available to all; so this gives us the courage to come before you. He used to impress upon us that this Yoga and the philosophy on which it is based — called the Advaita or non-dual philosophy — did not require to be reinforced by personal opinion, for it was revealed in the remote past by illumined men, who were sages, saints *and* psychologists as well...

The lectures in this book are given in this spirit, in the confidence that Yoga, when correctly and intelligently practised, can not only relieve human sufferings and frustrations, but lead to their ultimate transcendence.

INTRODUCTION

THERE IS a considerable interest in the subject of Yoga today, but a great deal of misunderstanding about it. The first thing to be understood, and which is not generally known, is that there are many Yogas, in fact as many as there are aspects of Christian religion. The word 'Yoga' literally means 'yoke' and the idea fundamentally is the pursuit of that which will link, yoke or unite the soul to Divinity.

To most people in the West, Yoga is a sort of magic that, if practised, will bring you powers to make money, to be healthy or perennially young, and in the popular mind it is associated with fakirs or Eastern people able to walk in the air, project their thoughts and have other occult powers. What has brought the word 'Yoga' into general disrepute is largely ignorance of the whole subject and the desire of the journalist to cater for sensationalism beloved of the masses. This is a pity, for the real Yoga is something very different and fundamentally spiritual.

Because the larger number live automatically rather than consciously, Hatha Yoga is the most widely known of all the Yogas. This is literally the control of the will by physical means, which involves breathing and other exercises combined with a rigid asceticism and should never be practised except under a trained instructor. In the East, this Yoga is considered to be of the lowest order and for those who have not yet learnt to control their instincts. Some of the easier exercises have filtered through to Westerners and are merely childish from the point of view of a true exponent; in any case they are all concerned with the body or physical sheath.

The more advanced Yoga can be called the science of control of the mind, or balanced living. It does not demand of its adherents the withdrawal from any orthodox creed; in fact you can belong to any belief you like and still take up Yoga. The East has always been much more universal in its outlook than the West and all Incarnations of God (*Avataras*), saints and prophets are equally revered. No Buddhist, for instance, has ever waged an aggressive war, for they do not believe in taking life in any form.

For the pursuit of the higher Yoga you have to understand something of your own make-up, and the traditional teachers are great psychologists. It is believed that the mind of man is merely an instrument, say, like a pen, which should be under the individual's complete control; but most people follow their minds like slaves and consequently alternate between joy and sorrow, being entirely at the mercy of their circumstances. This is called living automatically, and to live consciously you have to realize that the real 'I' of man is not the mind or the body which are subject to change and decay, but something entirely different standing behind the mind, able to direct it and a witness of its vagaries. You can prove this for yourself by reflecting that, when a child, you referred to yourself as 'I', when young also, and in old age as well, nor has that 'I' changed with the changes of the body. Your 'I' is not less because you lose a limb or more because you acquire wealth. That 'I' can say 'I won't think of that, it depresses me', 'I will think of so-and-so'; in other words, you are the *subject* of your mind and can control it, like a car. If you allow the mind to control you, you are allowing the car to take charge without any directing force.

Yoga consists in learning to control and direct the mind, tranquillizing it and rendering it completely obedient to the behests of the 'I'; but this is not all. When by various practices, of which meditation plays an important part, you have your mind under complete control, you become aware of much that was quite unknown to you before. A story in this connection may clarify this point. A rich man sent his boy to the native school where children repeat their lessons in chorus. When he visited the school, he complained that he could not hear his son and the boy was therefore not being taught properly. The teacher then silenced each child in turn, leaving only the rich man's son repeating the theme, and the father was satisfied.

Now, if we allow our minds to be in a constant state of agitation and Babel, so to speak, full of biases and prejudices, we fail to hear the voice of Truth that is submerged in this din. As we gain control of the mind, we become more and more aware of values that hitherto had not been able to reveal themselves to us. Every mystic will substantiate this, and for those who give themselves up to this life, one might well quote: 'Eye has not seen nor ear heard ... what has been prepared for them'.

Even a little of this practice of control of the mind brings enormous advantages, nor is it necessary to go to a forest or enter a cave to put it into practice. It can be inserted into one's ordinary routine, though, naturally, an hour or two daily must be devoted to the practices. One sees so much lack of satisfaction and strain in the world today and wonders why more people don't dig a little deeper to find a solution. There is no doubt, however, that those who take up the spiritual Yoga have peace, poise and something to put against fear and adversity. I have lived for years amongst them, and it is a unique and satisfying experience. If there is a purpose in life, and I am firmly convinced of this, they have found it.

I

THE MEANING OF YOGA

THE FIRST thing to say is that Yoga is neither a religion nor a philosophy, as we understand these terms in the West. It is a scientific spiritual training, coming down from the remote past, differing slightly to suit the different schools by which it is employed, but always the same in one particular, and that is that its goal is a spiritual one, and that goal is to enable the pupil to realize the divinity of his own true nature, and by this I mean, of course, to realize the divinity of the true nature of man. That is the goal and purpose of Yoga. The ancient teachers have said that the reason why man is in the world is that he may learn to know God, and Yoga affords the means which enables him to do so.

If anyone tells you that Yoga is a training whereby psychic powers are produced, or indeed any power is produced for its own sake, you may know for certain that he is speaking of a pseudo-Yoga, and not of one of the traditional and true Yogas.

Yoga is a spiritual training, so it goes without saying that it must be undertaken under the guidance of a recognized teacher. When I say 'a recognized teacher', I mean one who has received his permission to teach from a teacher who is himself in a recognized line of teachers. These teachers are few and far between and neither they nor their methods are easy to come by. One of the reasons that Yoga is sometimes discredited in both East and West is because unauthorized teachers and spurious Yogas are simply legion, and in this utility and synthetic age, more and more unpleasing and fantastic variants of Yoga are coming to the fore and often receiving serious attention.

Adhyatma Yoga teaches the ancient psychological practices whereby a man may make his return to God. First, he is taught how to control his instruments — the body, the mind and the emotions. When these have been stilled and really pacified, then his attention is directed to the super-conscious mind, the enlightened intellect, a force which is lying behind the work-a-day mind, dormant and unrecognized in most people, and which is the organ of spiritual perception.

The normal consciousness of man has been very well studied by educationalists and psychologists, and the subconscious mind is beginning to be explored and treated by the psychiatrists and psychoanalysts; but the ancient teachers both of the East and the West have always spoken of the existence of a super-conscious mind, and have laid down rules how to locate and use it.

I think you will agree that the saints have located and entered this sphere of consciousness, but it is the general opinion that only they can do so. Now what the great teachers of Yoga have maintained for hundreds, perhaps thousands of years, is that, far from being the prerogative of a few gifted souls, entrance into this region where divine knowledge can be obtained is the birthright of every man and woman who is willing to pay the price for it; that it is the natural and normal fulfilment of man's nature and therefore can be achieved in this very life.

Now the word 'price' has been used. Everything, spiritual as well as material, has its price, as every adult knows, and it is a blessing of God that this is so, for it is the only safeguard to the preservation of perfection in art, in craftsmanship, as well as in things spiritual. Only those reach perfection in any trade, art or science, who reverence perfection so much that they are willing to sacrifice for it. A poet has said: 'The heights attract but not the steps thereto!' Most of us want freedom from fear, from the domination of our individual personalities, and we all want *knowledge* — but not so many are willing to give what is demanded to achieve these things.

The price demanded is in the discipline laid down, and I will give you a very general idea of what this discipline involves so far as Yoga is concerned. First, the pupil must produce in himself a real desire to *know*. The spirit of experiment or curiosity will never draw out of anyone the necessary enthusiasm to support them through the hardships and difficulties which are always the natural accompaniment of learning anything. The desire to know can be stimulated by seeking the company of those who do know, at any rate *something* of the subject, and this is why societies and communities, though perhaps very trying to the individualist, are the best forcing houses for learning. The would-be pupil is advised to seek the company of those who know — the 'society of the good', it is called in the ancient classics. This is a preliminary measure which may or may not continue.

The second quality he must produce in himself is continuity of purpose, without which he can do nothing with himself nor can anyone do anything with him.

Then the would-be pupil must have sufficient

humility, or I prefer to call it self-knowledge, to put himself under a teacher, and the necessary faith and obedience to carry out that teacher's instructions to the letter. In all spiritual schools and very much so in Yoga, a great point is made of reverence. It is held that it indicates an absence of egoism and the presence of imagination in the pupil.

No one has ever seen a really good craftsman or artist who has not got a reverence for his art, his tools and, I think you will agree, reverence for the one who has taught him that art or craft. The imagination which recognizes another system of values, and the selflessness which enables the man to conform to that system, are very valuable characteristics in the make-up of any pupil.

Once my teacher's teacher, a great saint called Shri Dada, was sitting on the banks of the Ganges, and a man came up and asked him whether the mind developed gradually until it became enlightened, or whether the Truth broke on it suddenly — the Truth, that is, of the oneness of man and God. Shri Dada pointed to the steps leading from the water to a temple nearby and said:

> The first step is *faith*. The second step is *resolution*. The third: *sustained exertion*. The

fourth: *knowledge*. The fifth: *devotion*. The sixth: *self-surrender*. The seventh: *Self-realization*. He who practises these daily with zeal, will enter the Temple of Self-knowledge.

In one of the ancient scriptures, it says: 'Wonderful is the teacher, but wonderful, most wonderful is also the pupil'. I think he must be!

Now what does the teacher offer to the pupil from his side? Before all else he must have tried out and proved in his own experience the efficacy of the practices he gives to his pupils. He must teach and be an adept in the proven methods of meditation, and the exercises for obtaining control of the mind and the emotions. He must also be in a position to direct his pupils' studies, although he need not be a scholar or indeed what is usually known as a 'clever man'. Shri Dada, whom I mentioned just now, was no scholar at all and worked all day for his living in the telegraph office of the Indian railways. But the teacher, to be a real teacher, must also be a channel of God and so be able to advise the pupil from his higher intuitional knowledge, what to do and what to avoid doing. It goes without saying that, once chosen, he should be treated with the greatest respect and reverence.

There are, of course, many types of aspirants.

Some instinctively praise and worship God through their hearts and emotions. Some do so through their brains — through knowledge — and some through the work of their hands — through service. There are recognized Yogas to instruct each of these types and many more as well. There is *Bhakti Yoga*, the Yoga of devotion, in which the art of recollection and contemplation is the central teaching. *Jnana Yoga* is the Yoga of abstract knowledge and philosophy; and *Karma Yoga*, the Yoga of service. In this Yoga, every action is done to the glory of God and the results of all actions, good and bad, are offered to Him.

Adhyatma Yoga, which we study in Shanti Sadan, is made up of an admixture of these three Yogas — devotion, knowledge and service. It is held by the teachers in this Yoga that knowledge without devotion and service can be dry and theoretical; that service without knowledge and devotion can be a menace to society; and that devotion without knowledge and service often degenerates into fanaticism. We are therefore instructed to develop these three sides simultaneously.

The meaning of 'Adhyatma Yoga' is: 'That Yoga by means of which the supreme Reality,

God, is found (when the necessary knowledge and self-purification have been obtained) to be identical with the individual soul in man'. The belief standing behind this Yoga is non-duality: that is, the belief that God is the only Reality, and that everything which appears, stays for a time and disappears again, only does so by virtue of His continuous existence and all-pervading presence.

The great exponent of this Yoga is the mighty philosopher Shri Shankaracharya, and the Indian scripture called the *Bhagavad Gita* contains the practical exposition of its teachings. It has numbered countless sages and saints among its followers, as well as many of the rank and file of humanity for whom it is especially suitable on account of its practical teachings on action. Hari Prasad Shastri, the founder of Shanti Sadan, was a real exponent of Yoga and a very great scholar also.

II

WHAT YOGA HAS TO OFFER

THIS TALK proposes to set out some of the boons which Yoga has to offer to an aspirant, and, perhaps a more important point, what steps the aspirant will have to take to fit himself to receive these gifts. The success of a venture, spiritual or worldly, is dependent to a large extent on preparation and, even before preparation has started, on a preliminary research into the real nature of the objective.

Is the objective what it appears to be? How much energy, time and equipment will it cost us to achieve it? What will be gained when the goal has been reached? These are questions which might be asked by any mountaineer before he starts on an important climb. Not only must he acquaint himself with the lie of the land, from maps and information received from others who have already attempted the climb, but he will most certainly try to take a look at the peak from a distance, before he begins the ascent. George Mallory, who was on two of the early Everest expeditions, used to tell how they gazed at the mountain from all angles, when weather permitted, focusing all their experience and imagination upon it, until they thought that they had in fact climbed it successfully. To visualize success and not failure is a wise move in the preparation for any venture.

As the preliminary investigations are so very important, I will repeat what I have already said. There are three stages in the preparation before embarking on any project: (1) What is the goal? (2) Do I want to achieve it and if so, why? (3) What sacrifices and steps will I have to take to attain it?

We will now consider these questions with reference to the spiritual science of Yoga. Why do I want to make a research into Yoga? Is it in order to collect fresh facts and theories as a squirrel collects nuts? Do I want to know in order to be able to get more out of the life I lead at present? Or do I desire to serve an apprenticeship and make sacrifices in order to be introduced to something completely new and emancipating? Am I an adventurer, a business man or an explorer? Is it curiosity, ambition or a true desire for knowledge which actuates me? Some, when they recognize the grandeur and challenge of an idea or a thing, seek identification with it for its own sake. Others are already so completely identified with their art, profession or trade, or the money and power these produce, that they only seek information on other subjects in order to increase this identification. Such a man asks about every new thing: 'Will it fit me more completely for my work in life?', while the man in the first category says: 'I'll just see what it is all about'.

Now to answer some of the questions we have raised. We need not bother very much about the curiosity hunter, the one after exciting short cuts, for he is never in the same place or after the same thing for very long. But the other two, the man who wants to know whether Yoga will help him to get power, renown, or to run his business, and the man who wants to get out of his present restrictions and into a new realm of thought and being — they have to be answered.

It may not seem so at first sight, but these two types of men have one factor in common — the desire for expansion and satisfaction. Our teacher has said that man is an exile from his home, and his every action, worldly or otherwise, is an effort to return to where he belongs. Even the drunkard drinks because it gives him a temporary sense of expansion and makes him forget for a time his circumstances and his difficulties. But then why should this be so desirable, why can't he be satisfied with his life as it is? The Yoga says that it is because man is in fact, though unknown to himself, a king, and that his mind is after kingly pleasures and unlimited sovereignty; it is not after the pleasures of the mob. There are some words about this by Prince Dara Shikoh, son of the Mogul Emperor Shah Jahan, who built the Taj Mahal. He says:

> The essence of man has entered this framework of the body, so that the seed of perfection which lies in him latent may become patent, that what is in potentiality may become actuality.

You may say: 'Well, it's a pleasant theory but no more'. But the philosophy of Vedanta also deals with this assertion, not in symbolic language but in philosophical axioms, and the answer comes out the same. Hidden behind the limited personality there is limitless consciousness and unwearying power. The revealed scriptures of the *Upanishads* say, *Ayam Atma Brahma* — which means 'This Self, my innermost Self, the Self of each and everyone, is God or *Brahman*'. They also say, *Kham Brahman* — 'All is God'. This Self or God, being infinite and all pervasive, it therefore follows that man must also be infinite and all bliss by nature. This truth was seen by the sages of the past, and it is the first and greatest boon which the Advaita philosophy has bestowed on the world. It is the liberating truth, the knowledge which brings peace and bliss, and the life of man is spent, consciously or unconsciously, in trying to bring it to realization within himself. Even when he is experimenting and struggling, alternately suffering and enjoying in the world, he is instinctively trying, often blindly and mistakenly, to free himself *from* the world, from its limitations of multiplicity and change. When the time comes for these efforts to be made consciously, he will probably seek the company of others on the same quest, and enter the path of discipleship and learning.

Before this truth can become a liberating force, however, the aspirant must test it for himself. He must test it in three ways: philosophically, experimentally and intuitionally. The process by which this is done is called Yoga. These tests are, at the same time, ways of research and ways of training.

The first test is philosophical, not in the highest sense of the word, but in so far as it is an enquiry and research by the mind into the written word and transmitted truth. According to the ancient teachers, this enquiry, this search into the doctrine, and the capacity to learn and retain the teachings, is the first prerequisite of all pupils. They must desire to know, they must make sacrifices in order to know and they must ponder on what they have learnt and remember it. This quality is called *vichara* in Sanskrit, the unprejudiced, careful and reverent study of the data which has been collected on the subject, and the listening with an open mind to the truth when it is imparted by word of mouth by one who knows. The practice of *vichara* includes the study of traditional works on the philosophy such as the *Bhagavad Gita, The Crest Jewel of Discrimination, Direct Experience of Reality* and other works which will be recommended by those who have benefited from their study.

Keeping in mind that this is one of the modes of verification, the aspirant is sure to have, and indeed he should hope to have, many queries and doubts as he proceeds with his investigation. Dr Shastri used to welcome such questions, but he counselled pupils to make it a rule to have only one well formulated doubt at a time, and to deal with it exhaustively. Even more important, to look on a doubt as a doubt and not as a settled conclusion.

The next realm of research, and it is to be

engaged in at the same time as enquiry, is experiment or practice. This is an approach where all meet at the beginning to have a good time, for nearly everyone enjoys putting a theory into practice and seeing if it works. Through the traditional practices of meditation and mind control, which are available to all, the pupil now begins to realize that there is a factor within him which is independent of the body and the mind, and that it can become the observer and master of them both.

Once this possibility has been envisaged, the aspirant has received notice of the second great boon transmitted to him by the great teachers of the past, the knowledge that his true Self is independent of the body and the mind and can direct them both. This knowledge, if constantly kept before him, prevents the pupil from thinking that it is he who is suffering from limitations which are, in fact, lodged in his mental and physical instruments. We must, however, go warily with this idea. Our teacher used to warn us that Truth is a dangerous weapon if misused. It is like a knife. You can cut your bonds with it or you can cut your throat. This knowledge does not mean that the pupil disclaims henceforward all responsibility and watches things take their course. A man is independent of his car, but if it is showing a fault, he will have to correct it before he can proceed on his journey. Detachment from the mind and body lessens fear and the sense of inferiority, for if you are convinced that you are intrinsically far greater than you appear to be, it does give you courage to face difficulties and overcome them.

Dr Shastri used to tell a story to illustrate this. Apparently, until the beginning of this century, a Mohammedan was considered, in India, to be the physical superior of a Hindu. One day two youths, one a Hindu and the other a Mohammedan, fell into a quarrel which led to blows. The Hindu threw the violent, uncontrolled Mohammedan and sat proudly on his chest. The Mohammedan said: 'Yes, you have beaten me. Of what caste are you?' 'I'm a shopkeeper', replied the Hindu. The Mohammedan gave one strong blow to the face of the triumphant youth and in an instant was upon him, crying, 'What! A shopkeeper overthrow a Mohammedan? It's impossible, a contemptible Hindu overcome a Moslem, a true believer!' He had remembered his superior nature and was easily the victor.

Dr Shastri used to say, after telling this story: Think always, 'I am not the body, I am not the mind. I am Truth, I am Reality'.

Now to go back to experiment. As you may expect, the prime object for experiment is the mind. Our teacher used to say, 'A cat has nine lives but the mind has nine hundred or even more!' So you may guess that this field of experiment is more a field of battle than a quiet laboratory of research!

According to the Vedanta psychology the mind is, in itself, inert and unconscious, being composed of inert matter. Its apparent and constant movement is the result of its proximity to the great force of Consciousness behind it. It has no power of movement of its own, its chief characteristic being that it mirrors that with which it is brought into contact. Thus it is likened to a crystal which takes on the colour of the object against which it is set, or to a sponge which soaks up and pours forth the liquid into which it has been immersed. When it has not yet been controlled and directed, it directs and controls its owner. But, nevertheless, its true function is to be the medium through which both God *and* the world are reflected. Therefore, its control and direction is the central point in the Yoga training.

From what has been said, it will be seen that the mind is not naturally either trivial or holy. It is not naturally anything except receptive, but due to its juxtaposition to multiplicity and the sense objects, its atmosphere is only too often diffused and trivial. A walk down a London street, or only a few minutes in a tube lift, surrounded by advertisements of Brylcreem and various articles of clothing, can leave the untrained mind restless and beset by lowering forces.

The object of the discipline is to slow down the aimless activity of the mind by interrupting its contact with the sense objects and concepts, and placing near it the antidote of wisdom, which means, at this stage, a growing knowledge of the spiritual philosophy, a recognition of the nature of the world of phenomena, and an awareness of the awakening power behind it. This will expand and tranquillize the mind and enable it to reflect, in time, the light of consciousness behind it.

It is told of a certain king of ancient India, that when he was holding his court, he used to amuse himself by putting difficult problems to his ministers and watching their confusion. One day he caused a long line to be drawn on a wall in front of them, and then called on anyone to shorten it without touching or changing the line in any way. They were all perplexed, as he had hoped they would be, and no one moved, until suddenly his chief adviser stepped forward and drew a longer line beside it. This is exactly what happens to the mind during training. Attention is not directed to the mind itself; but those things which have an expanding and eternal quality are placed beside it, and it ceases to rule the scene.

Now this process of placing the longer line beside the mind is the technique of meditation and also of contemplation of those qualities which have a releasing power. In the initial stages of their training, the Buddhists contemplate and repeat the names of such characteristics as 'courage', 'compassion', 'fearlessness' and so on, for to ponder on them expands the mind and breaks down its adhesions. But the chief technique for transforming, raising and tranquillizing the mind is the practice of meditation.

Our teacher has said that meditation without a spiritual purpose is of little value. Its true aim should be to gain a knowledge of the Truth, not to obtain control of the mind. In fact, he used to say that *per se,* meditation was valueless and that its real value lay in its being the method whereby the knowledge of God is attained. But a realization of this fact does not come at once; only experience will confirm it. Here again, in the early stages of training, preparation is almost as important as the actual meditation itself; for unless the mind has been quietened before starting, what will happen to the unfortunate meditator? Wherever anything lasting and valuable is to be effected, some degree of creative power should be present, and you must be something of a creative artist when preparing for meditation. In fact, it is during the preparation and not during the performance of meditation that the creative imagination must be brought into play. When the actual meditation starts, quite other powers come to the surface.

The first creative act in the preparation is to produce an atmosphere in which the mind feels expanded and at peace, a scene in which the meditation can take place. Our teacher once described for our benefit one of these visualizations. It was a scene in the high Himalayas, the half moon hanging in a clear sky over the silent and majestic peaks, revealing range after range. You are there alone, at one with that beauty. This visualization, he said, would drive away the anxieties, trivialities and interests of the world, and prepare the mind to feel the breath of spiritual infinitude, when the real meditation started. Each one of us must set the stage for themselves. Some prefer to imagine themselves in the presence of a saint of God, and to do the meditation before him. Others can fill their mind with an abstract concept and it becomes all light, while some have simply to remain still and think of a name of God, *Om* or Jesus, Rama or Krishna. But in the beginning it is not wise to sit down unprepared and try to plunge the mind into meditation.

Another creative act which must be practised is reverence. It may seem strange that this quality is creative and can be consciously produced, but Dr Shastri has said that both reverence and devotion must be cultivated, for they are not natural to every man. Reverence is the outcome of a recognition by a mind made sensitive by imagination, of qualities in an object or concept which are higher than it can as yet produce in itself. Thus a most important preliminary to the practice of meditation is to affirm the existence, and then the presence, of some great Being or some great Power, and then to place the mind beside it, in order that it may open itself, in worship and reverence. Control of the mind is less important at this juncture than this attitude of reverence. Even if, after all this, the mind fails to remain in real meditation even for a few seconds, some of its adhesions will have been broken down by this practice. Every time this attitude of reverence is produced, the personality or inner atmosphere of the mind begins to undergo a change. A new habit, a spiritual one, is being formed. Everyone knows to his cost how hard it is to break bad habits, but it is also hard to break new ones, and once they have been established, a great advance has been made.

Now begins the highest stage of research, the intuitional verification. Our teacher taught that there is a faculty of illumination in every mind which is not aroused until certain practices have been carried out. Consciousness, which has so far been the cause of the movement, energy and quality of its medium, the mind, and through which it has fractionally manifested itself, now experiences itself through no medium — it knows itself by its own light. Intuition is knowing directly and not through a process, and at the stage we are now speaking of, intuition is beginning to usurp the functions of the mind. But this stage is a very high one and is not for our seeker as yet, so we will leave him nearing the crest of his mountain and return for a moment to the practical man.

A certain detachment and a growth of fearlessness comes from even a slight interest in the yogic teachings and a little practice of mind control and short meditations. To repeat such words as, 'courage', 'compassion', 'fearlessness', and to meditate on their meaning and to feel they are growing within, is a good practice. Above all, try sometimes to go where the teachings of Vedanta and Yoga are discussed, to read the classics on the subject and to acknowledge that there are more things in heaven and earth than are dreamt of in any philosophy. All this links the aspirant with the infinite and abstract Power, and his mind will slowly expand and change under its creative light .

I will now give a short summary of what has been said. The Vedanta has three great gifts to give its followers. The first is the knowledge *Brahman satyam jagan mithya,* 'God alone is real, the rest unreal, and God and man are one'. This knowledge brings permanent release from bondage when it is directly realized. The second gift is the knowledge 'I am not the body or the mind. I am the witness of both and I can control them'. This knowledge gives fearlessness and detachment. The third gift is the knowledge that one consciousness pervades all, therefore all living beings are one and belong to one family. This belief brings a pure selfless life.

The truth of these three statements must be

tested and proved before they can become lights to light the way of the pupil. The ways by which these truths are verified are philosophical, experimental and intuitional, and to give the technique by which these experiments are conducted is the function of Yoga.

III

THE PSYCHOLOGY OF YOGA

YOGA IS a system of psychological training designed to effect changes in the *antahkarana* or inner being of man, as a result of which he is made aware of, and then learns how to awaken and put to use, the powers lying dormant behind his conscious mind. This leads him to an understanding of the truth about his own nature, a realization of the all-pervadingness of God, and finally to a direct perception of the identity of his Self and God. In fact Yoga may be said to be primarily the science of the search for God, and secondly the science of wise action based on a mastery of the body, mind and emotions.

The training is both spiritual and psychological. The great *rishis* or seers of the past, who 'saw' in their illumined understanding the truth concerning the relationship of God, man and the cosmos, laid down certain rules and discipline which are followed by every aspirant. They ordained that when the preliminary self-purification had been effected, each pupil should conduct his own researches and substantiate for himself the claims made by those who direct him.

These claims are unequivocal and do not vary. They assert that the so-called ordinary or normal man is only twenty-five per cent alive, and that while he is in this condition it is impossible for him to know the true and innate divinity of his nature. At the same time, it is claimed that every man has it in his power to develop his faculties to their fullest extent, and so reach maturity and liberation in this very life. This end is achieved through a patient and obedient carrying out of the injunctions of the teacher, by study and by companionship with the like-minded.

No-one can be given the title of Guru or spiritual teacher unless he is in the pure tradition and has himself been the accepted disciple of a Guru. Not only must he have been the disciple of an accepted teacher, but he must have satisfied him and have received from him the mandate to teach. He must be familiar with the difficulties and dangers of the way, and he is treated with the greatest reverence and obedience by his pupils. Although it is not essential for him to be a scholar, yet, by virtue of his enlightened understanding, he will be able to instruct his pupils in the traditional groundwork of the philosophy he represents. Later, those of his disciples who wish to pursue the path of knowledge, will be accepted by pundits for advanced instruction on the recommendation of his name alone.

Yoga being a scientific system of training, it may well be asked what part of man's being it is that is subjected to this training and discipline and what form it takes. The answer is that the entire inner organ is brought under scrutiny, then controlled and purified, and finally used as the medium through which the final illumination which brings liberation is attained. The words 'brought under scrutiny' mean that the pupil's attention is directed by the teacher to the fact that he possesses an instrument which records perceptions and conceptions and which is not only the seat of the emotions, will and memory, but is at the same time the ground for their play. This instrument is called in Sanskrit the *antahkarana*, the mind or inner organ, in contra-distinction to the outer organ, or body.

Yoga psychology holds the *antahkarana* to be a nucleus through which the localized consciousness has access to the world of phenomena by means of the sense organs. It is called the eleventh sense. The knowledge of objects is said to be obtained through the *antahkarana*, for, as consciousness, it contacts objects, classifies and dissects them, and then relates them to the ego, or sense of 'I-ness' in man. It is made up of four aspects: *manas*, *buddhi*, *chitta* and *ahankara*. The *manas* corresponds to our conception of the perceptive powers of the normal or lower mind, which recognizes and classifies percepts and concepts in succession. It then presents its findings to the individual sense, the 'I', known as *ahankara*, and at the same time the faculty of discriminating knowledge comes into operation. This faculty is called *buddhi*, or the reason, higher and lower. The *chitta* is the sense of emotion and memory and produces the individual background which colours the findings of the lower *buddhi* or reason in each case.

This central nucleus of consciousness is in a constant state of tension and activity in the untrained man. It is maintained as a medium by virtue of its recognition of diversity and the qualities which it reveals to itself as hidden in phenomena and to which it reacts with pleasure or aversion. It is the medium for knowledge and also for desire, and the ground on which the play of the pairs of opposites is carried on.

The object of the Yoga training is to turn the consciousness which is the *antahkarana* from streaming outwards to contact phenomena, and direct it inwards to contact its essence or substratum; to so control it that it sees unity where it formerly saw diversity. This is done, as has already been explained, by the practice of meditation and contemplation, by absorbed listening to the truth and by the repetition of a holy Name. These practices produce ascendency over the activities of the mind, a state of independence of sense data, through the continuous consideration and recognition of unity.

In order that a decentralization of consciousness shall take place, the practice of ignoring multiplicity and contemplating unity must be carried on beyond the hours of meditation and study. This is why the practice of Yoga has been named from time immemorial 'the science of wise living'. When the meditative habit has been formed and the consciousness has, so to say, turned upon itself as the ever-present unitive substratum of phenomena, the arousing of the intuitive consciousness begins, and the disciple may be said to be advancing in Yoga.

The discovery of the independence of the Self, the central Consciousness or Spirit, of its instrument, the localized consciousness, and its power over it, is brought about by the Guru in ways which cannot be set out here, but always in conjunction with the discipline of control and purification. For without such discipline, the theoretical knowledge of the extreme independence of the Self would prove a danger to the pupil and to those around him. When the preliminary discipline and practice of regarding the *antahkarana* objectively has been mastered, the pupil will have a good working idea of its capacity for endurance, for abstract thinking, for receiving and assimilating impressions and knowledge, for emotion, for will and dedication to an ideal. He now knows that his mind has not only the power to criticize, dissect and think, but also the power to choose what to think about.

When he knows this through experiment and continuous watchfulness, he may be said to be conversant with the workings of his mind, but he cannot yet be said to know how to control or purify it. A man may be an able mechanic and no driver. In the *Katha Upanishad,* one of the most ancient of the Eastern scriptures, it says: 'No-one whose senses are unpurified and not under control, and whose mind is not collected and at rest, can acquire knowledge of the Spirit'.

It is not within the scope of this talk to describe in detail the steps by which purification and control of the *antahkarana* is achieved. It is sufficient to say that once the instrument has been brought into focus and examined, so to say, it is essential that it should be cleansed and controlled if it is to be of any use and not a source of danger. A knowledge of the component parts of the *antahkarana* is a very great asset, but the ideal for which it is ultimately to be sacrificed will not attract unless a high degree of purification has been achieved.

Hearing the truth, called *shravana*; brooding on the truth heard, called *manana*; continued contemplation of the truth, called *nididhyasana*; together with dedication of the thoughts, words and deeds to an *Avatara*, a saint of God or the teacher, are the ways which lead to purification and control, and they require separate and careful explanation elsewhere.

To sum up: The aim of the Yoga training is to cause the pupil:

1. to realize that activity is a localized phenomenon, and is not an attribute of his innate spirit.
2. to bring the field of that activity into focus, and to teach him to control it.
3. to purify and direct the *antahkarana,* and finally to bring its activities to a standstill by unveiling the unchanging and ever-satisfying

Consciousness to its view.

4. to disintegrate and dissolve the localized consciousness into the cosmic Consciousness.

It will be noted that nothing has been said of the part played by divine grace in this miracle of the transmutation of the *antahkarana*, or of the fructifying power of devotion. Just as tillage goes on in the open air, under the light and power of the sun's rays, so the husbandry of Yoga proceeds to its culmination under the light and protection of divine Consciousness. When man has done his part, there is nothing left for him to do but to wait, like the silent fields, until the sun and rain of grace brings on his harvest.

IV

THE INNER DISCIPLINE OF YOGA

THE GREAT philosopher Shri Shankara defines the word 'Adhyatma' as 'that which is at first known as the soul in the body, but which, in the end, is found to be identical with the supreme Reality — God'. The word 'Yoga' means a yoke, not in the sense of something which restrains, but in the sense of something which joins. Adhyatma Yoga, the Yoga of Self-knowledge, is therefore a metaphysical Yoga, having as its goal the realization of man's identity with God or Truth. In the traditional Yogas, there is no training given in occult or psychic practices, for the goal is always a spiritual one. In fact, a true Yoga may be said to be a science which teaches the way of approach, or rather the way of return, to God.

There are many paths by which a man may return to God. Some take the path of knowledge, some of devotion, and others of disciplined and selfless action, and there are Yogas which deal with each of these paths. Adhyatma Yoga gives training in the three paths of devotion, action or service, and knowledge. According to its teachings, the pupil must aim to become proficient in all three, and it is considered important that during his training at least, he should look on them all with an equal eye.

In the *Bhagavad Gita*, which is one of the great scriptures of the world and a mine of wisdom about Yoga, it is said that Yoga teaches inner equilibrium — that is, perfect co-ordination between the Spirit and the instruments. In this balance lies the secret of right and constructive action and it can only be attained when the disciple has learnt to live as a guest in his mind and body, so to say, and does not allow himself to be imprisoned in them and subject to their fluctuations. This is a very difficult thing to achieve, but it is an important aspect of the teaching, inasmuch as it paves the way to detachment and gives freedom from the burden of likes and dislikes.

In this Yoga, the outer life of action and the inner state of meditation are looked on as inter-dependent. The quality of a meditation which lasts one hour is largely determined by the quality of the life one lives when not in meditation. Conversely, the daily life will not be vital and constructive unless it is fed and based on meditation and communion with God. A modern *rishi* has said: 'It is foolishness to bar your doors and windows against the ravaging thief for one hour, and to leave them open for twenty-three. You will surely lose your treasure'.

In order to live constructively, a man must bring the same qualities to bear on his active life as he brings to his meditation and study. What qualities must he try to cultivate if he is to gain the mastery over both worlds in the end? To begin with, two fundamental ones, the second growing out of the first: *desire* and *devotion*. Somehow or other he has got to awaken an ardent and sustained desire to know, to experience, and to transcend his work-a-day self. If he can awaken this desire, devotion will come of its own accord. This is the fire which cooks the meal; without it, all the virtues will remain tasteless and useless.

This desire is really present in man from the beginning. It is evidence of his divine nature, but while he is in the elementary stage of development, it manifests as the instinctive urge to expand materially, to acquire possessions, wealth and fame, and to experience all the worldly pleasures. The first evidence of inner growth comes when, as a result of repeated disappointments and painful experiences, this urge ceases to be instinctive, and becomes a conscious decision to make inner instead of outer explorations.

Once he has reached this stage, let the man seek association with the spiritually mature or, at least, with those who are more advanced in the search than he is. St Augustine says that 'one loving spirit sets another on fire', and it is very true. If he cannot have association with spiritual men, then let him read the words of the saints and think over their lives, for the mind takes on the colour of what it thinks upon, and in time, its rhythm changes also.

Dr Shastri used to say that man has two ways of learning open to him. One is to be taught slowly, by nature, and the other is to be taught quickly by the saints, teachers and scriptures. When the Truth or spiritual knowledge is given by the teachers, it is not imparted by the tongue; it passes most secretly and swiftly, and its reception is attended by great inner changes. Indeed, only by results is its presence made known. The fact that the Truth has been grasped by the mind, is no evidence that it has been received into the inner being. In the *Chandogya Upanishad*, a teacher, speaking of this passing of knowledge and the transformation it effects, says: 'If you were to impart this to a dry stick, branches would grow and leaves spring from it'.

Once the desire and enthusiasm for knowledge has been awakened and the man is actively seeking out those who know, one may almost say that they will seek him out, and when the two sides meet, the transference will begin, drop by drop at first, and then in a steady stream. Discipline and fixity of purpose will help him at this stage, for discipline can develop most things. Discipline is a word much disliked and out of fashion today, for it suggests restraint and involves obedience. In reality, discipline is not coercion; it is the passing of a technique by one who has the authority of experience to one who recognizes that authority and is obedient to it. This recognition must be present, otherwise discipline is Dead Sea fruit.

There are certain other qualities which the teachers of all spiritual schools have considered to be essential in a pupil before he may receive the higher teachings. Our teacher placed complete harmlessness in thought, word and deed, first. This attitude springs from a recognition of the spiritual law of the universality of consciousness, which lays down that one Spirit pervades the whole creation. Consequently, all living beings, having this Spirit as their substratum, are interconnected. Man is not an independent unit and what he does will affect not only himself, but will have a universal significance. Before he has achieved a partial recognition of this truth, even spiritual power can be a source of danger in his hands.

After harmlessness and the desire and enthusiasm to know, there must be patient cultivation of reverence and devotion. Reverence opens man's shut doors. The true artist, the scientist and the saint, all reverence the object of their search. As reverence increases, the taint of egoity decreases, and the transmission of beauty and knowledge is made more possible. In the great Persian classic, the *Mathnawi*, it says:

> Dost thou know why the mirror of thy soul reflects nothing? It is because the rust is not cleared from its face.

The rust is egoity.

> How should a rock be covered with verdure by the Spring? Become earth, that thou mayest grow flowers of many a hue. For years thou hast been a heart-jagging rock. Once, for the sake of experiment, be earth.

Reverence precedes devotion and will produce it. Our teacher has said that both reverence and devotion can be consciously cultivated like any other qualities. Many say: 'Oh! I have no devotion, so these things are not for me.' But in this Yoga, devotion is not synonymous with emotion; it is recognized to be that which causes you to bring the mind again and again to the target; and love, when it is born, manifests to the yogi as a recognition of basic unity with the thing sought. If you learn to reverence and recognize the essence of anyone, or any thing for that matter, you will come to love its form in the end. Thus, unless the essence of the Vedanta is sensed and reverenced, you will never achieve a living relationship with its outer structure.

To love a physical form, you do not need to be an expert anatomist, nor do you need to be a philosopher or a logician to love the fundamental tenets of Adhyatma Yoga. What you do need is a selfless and devoted attention and a willingness to be transformed by the object of your attention. In one of his works, St Augustine puts these words into the mouth of the Lord:

> I am the food of the full-grown. Grow, and then thou shalt feed on Me, nor shalt thou change Me into thy substance as thou changest the food to thy flesh, but thou shalt be changed into Mine.

Harmlessness, a sense of urgency to know, the

cultivation of reverence and devotion, and only after all these have been achieved comes open-handed giving of the fruits of experience and research to anyone who is in need of them. In order to give — to do what is called 'good' — one must have a surplus out of which to give. 'No burdened one shall bear another's burden', says Rumi, the author of the *Mathnawi*, and surely the criticism of egoism and selfishness which is levelled against those who undertake a spiritual training to rid themselves and others of their burdens, is unfair. Spiritual wealth has to be amassed like any other wealth and should be freely shared when obtained; but a bankrupt cannot be a giver.

This is, in broad outline, the inner discipline of this Yoga or of any other spiritual school. What is the purpose of it all? That a man shall cease to be a slave of circumstance and become master of himself and live according to the divine principle within him, which will only reveal itself when he has acquired a pure enough vision — *that* is the purpose. The Lord does not need any assistance from us in order to permeate our being, but man must refine his senses if he is to become aware of this communication and this is the purpose of the yogic training. Music is permeating the atmosphere all the time, but the would-be listener will only hear it if he manipulates a radio correctly. To do this from a yogic point of view, he must learn to understand and manipulate his radio — the mind.

In order to live a dedicated life, you do not need to retire from the world, but you do need to live a retired life, by which I mean an unattached life. Retirement is a question for the mind, not the body. It has always been the hallmark of the great Adhyatma yogis that they can live and work in the world concealing their spiritual eminence from all except their equals and their personal disciples. Shri Dadaji, the Guru of our teacher, was a railway official, and his fellow workers simply knew him as a good man; only his disciples knew him for what he was — an illumined man.

Now a brief explanation of the teachings of this Yoga on the mind and its powers. We are told that man is born a builder. He must act and therefore he must build, and he will either build an invisible temple or he will build fetters for himself. It has been said that the craving for expansion was implanted in his heart in order that *that* which is within him might come into view, and so it is. He reproduces his inner activity — his thoughts and his desires — in an outer form.

'What a man thinks, that he becomes'. If he fills his mind with cinema sins, he will inevitably become as artificial as they are, and if he thinks with imagination and identification on the lives of the great saints and sages, his life will become creative and change its rhythm.

It is of course a platitude to say that thought is a most powerful and creative force, but one of the definitions of a platitude is that it is a statement which has been made so often that the truth contained in it has been forgotten. Here are some words which are more compelling than platitudes on the power of thought. They are again from the *Mathnawi*:

> When you see that from a thought, every craft in the world arises and subsists; that houses, palaces and cities, mountains and plains and rivers, earth and ocean, as well as the sun and sky, derive their life from it as fishes from the sea — then why in your foolishness, O blind one, does the body seem to you a Solomon, and thought only an ant? To your eyes the mountains appear great. To you thought is like a mouse, and the mountain like a wolf. The material world in your eyes is awful and sublime, you tremble and are frightened at the clouds, the thunder and the sky; while, in regard to the world of Thought, O lower than an ass, you are as secure and indifferent as a witless stone. From ignorance you deem the

shadow to be the substance, hence to you the substance has become a plaything and of slight account. Wait till the day when that thought unfolds its wings without any veil. You will see neither the sky nor the stars, nor any existence but God — the One, the Living, the Loving.

The control and direction of thought, and therefore of action, results in what can be called 'introspective living', that is, a life which is based on the inner spiritual law. To live consciously is to have a sense of direction, a direction towards a goal. In Yoga this goal is liberation — liberation from the mortal nature and a recognition of the divine nature, and entrance into it. This conception is not, as is often thought, purely an Eastern ideal; it is found in some Western mystics as well. Meister Eckhart in one of his Sermons, makes the Lord say: 'I became man for you; if you do not become God for me, you do me wrong.' 'To become God' — this is the purpose for which man comes into the world, and he must fulfil that purpose.

The Yoga gives many practices which will hasten this end. It is recommended, for instance, that in order to free himself from the trammels of the world, a man should regard himself as a pilgrim throughout his life. A pilgrim sleeps, cooks his food, talks with his fellow pilgrims, but his heart is always set on his objective. Chaucer's pilgrims entertained each other with tales, but their real passion was Canterbury. So the yogi is taught to live among his fellows, mutually giving and receiving assistance, enjoying what comes, but using everything and every action he performs to help him towards his longed-for goal. The true pilgrim is a lesson in detachment and purpose, and so is the true yogi.

In order to become detached from anything, the mind, which is ever seeking expansion and fulfilment, must be convinced that it can obtain greater satisfaction from another source than the one from which it obtains its joy at present. Perfection is attained through a series of self-disgusts. Therefore, at the outset, we do violence to ourselves, in the sense that we restrain the mind and the emotions from their instinctive play, and bring them to bear on those things which are of good report. To read about the spiritually great ones of the earth and to ponder on their lives, accustoms the heart to bear their finer rhythm and reproduces in us the light with which their hearts were filled. In this way the focus is shifted and changes are brought about, which many think can only be produced by time and austerity.

In one of the *Upanishads* it describes a disciple who has undertaken such a training:

> Having settled down [meaning, having made his choice], let him study the Truth and sacrifice for the Truth. Henceforth he becomes another, his fetters are cut asunder, he knows no expectation, no fear from others, as little from himself.

When you think of the postures, incantations and practices of some Yogas, such a discipline seems almost too simple; but this is a delusion, I can assure you!

A true teacher does not give information to his disciple; he effects a transformation in him, but only after that disciple has embraced the traditional discipline, and thus purified himself. When he first comes before his teacher, the world seems very real to him, and God, or *Brahman* only a name, a conception to which he clings in times of danger, or when there is something desirable to be obtained. When the teacher has finished with him, the position is reversed. The world now seems to be an appearance, a name, and God alone the reality. About such a transformation, St Augustine says: 'If you have received well, you are that which you have received'. In order to 'receive well', all preconceived notions of what is to be received, of how the teachings will be given and of what constitutes teaching will have to be abandoned. 'Come what may' is the watchword, and 'I will trust Thee even if Thou slayest me', the cry of the true disciple.

There is an old story which tells how a teacher and his disciple were on pilgrimage, and in the heat of the day they sat down in the shade to rest. Soon the disciple fell asleep with his head in the lap of the teacher. While he was sleeping peacefully, the teacher saw a large and poisonous snake approaching and preparing to attack his sleeping pupil. He begged the snake to show mercy and the snake, as is the custom of birds, beasts and reptiles in legends, understood his words and promised faithfully to depart, if he could have a drop of the pupil's blood, drawn from the throat. Quickly the teacher drew his knife and poised it over the throat of his disciple. At this moment, the boy opened his eyes and saw his teacher with the knife pointed at his throat. Looking at him with love and trust, the disciple smiled, closed his eyes and fell asleep again, and the snake departed, having received its toll of blood.

According to the teachers of this Yoga, there are three main stages on the spiritual path. They are three states of awareness, three aspects of the yogic life. First, the disciple sees himself as an apparently free unit, an independent body, but since he has already entered on the spiritual quest and it is his discipline to serve, he serves with that body. Next, he realizes that he is not independent, but a spark of the divine fire, an emanation from a Source, dependent on that Source and impelled by it, and, as that spark, he says he will burn and shine. Lastly he knows, by direct experience, that he is one with that Source, that he himself is the Source of all light, and as that Light he will cease *doing*, he will simply *be*. The first two states are preparations for the third. In fact, Yoga is the preparation made by man to enable him to reach this state of certainty. When it is reached, then Yoga is laid aside, for all systems have been transcended, and the man has become what is known as a *jivan-mukta*, one who has realized his Godhead in this very life — one whose highest activity is now *being*, not *doing*.

When the disciple has reached his goal, how does he live? Does he cut himself off from the world and retire into a cave to meditate? In the tradition of Adhyatma Yoga, these enlightened ones become as torches in the darkness to light their fellow men. Shri Shankara travelled all over India, teaching, dictating his commentaries and founding the four great monasteries in the four corners of India, two of which are still active. Shri Dadaji, Swami Mangalnathji, Swami Nirbhayanandaji — all modern *jivan-muktas* of this Yoga — worked and taught until they passed from this world. In the words of a Zen text:

> None knows of their inner life; they go into the market place and consort with wine-bibbers and butchers, and light the light under which all become Buddhas.

Many think that the supreme consummation of life is union with the Lord Incarnate as Rama, Krishna or Christ, or with a saint of God. This may be the consummation of experience, but the true consummation is other than this. It is a direct knowledge that there is no power outside yourself with whom to unite, that there is only One without a second, no other, and that 'That Thou Art'.

Some imagine, perhaps one should say, some fear, that when this stage is reached — a state where all individual progress is at an end and fulfilment has produced inner stillness and waveless consciousness — man enters a void, and that what is known in the Buddhist scriptures as *nirvana*, and in this Yoga as *nirvikalpa samadhi*, is in fact a nothingness. One can be certain that this state would never have been called 'the highest state' if it were a void, a vacuum, or a nullity. The illumined sages have testified that it is a fullness and a fulfilment.

The supreme Consciousness ever pervades all, and is the support of all multiplicity and unity, being and becoming. The apparent emptiness is in fact fullness, and forms the ground for the play of the world-drama, *maya*. The teachings of Advaita Vedanta affirm that this seeming emptiness is the hub of the three worlds and the cause of their fascination and power. Here description and words must end, for this state is hidden from our reason and the senses. Still, the great ones who have realized it are compassionate and try to give some indication of its nature through stories and symbols. In the *Chandogya Upanishad*, a Guru is trying to reveal to his disciple the fact of this supreme state. He tells his pupil to fetch him a fruit from the *nyagrodha* tree. When the boy has brought the fruit, he is asked what he sees within it. He answers that he sees extremely fine seeds. He is then told to break one of these and describe what he finds within. 'I find nothing at all, Venerable Sir'. The teacher says: 'My dear, that subtle essence which you do not perceive, verily, my dear, by reason of that very essence does this great *nyagrodha* tree exist. Believe me, my dear, that which is the subtle essence, in it the whole world has its Self. That is the true, That is the Self and That thou art, O Shvetaketu!'

In the West they also use symbols to describe the indescribable. 'There is in God, some say, a deep but dazzling darkness', writes Henry Vaughan, and that mystic who is called Dionysius the Areopagite talks of the 'radiance of the divine darkness' and says:

> We pray that we may come into that darkness which is beyond light; and that we may see and know, without seeing and knowing, that which is beyond vision and knowledge.

Reason turns away here, but at the point of contact in the high *samadhi*, or at the moment of grace, the soul of man intuitively recognizes that the end of its quest has come, and knowing this One-without-a-second to be its own Self, in that moment it loses its finitude in identity.

V

AFFIRMATIONS UNDERLYING YOGA

THE SPIRITUAL affirmations which underlie this Yoga are tremendous and startling. If they awaken immediate antagonism in you, or shock you, this Yoga is very probably not for you at present. But if they arouse a feeling of awe, or even of curiosity, prepare to make the spiritual experiments which will prove their truth to you.

The word 'affirmation' is used rather than 'philosophy', because philosophy to us has a very different meaning from the meaning it bears in the East. Here, the popular conception of philosophy is that it is a mental approach to fundamental questions, such as the nature of God and the soul, the nature of good and evil, and the goal of life; and that the answers to these problems which it supplies must be based on and supported by reason and logic. The activity is mental; devotion and reverence are not characteristics expected of a philosopher. No-one would look for a saint among the followers of Bergson or Bertrand Russell.

In the East, on the contrary, the questions considered are the same, but the answers to them are obtained, not by reasoning, but by direct spiritual experience. In other words, those philosophers who have influenced thought in the East, have been seers, saints and the trainers of saints as well. Their opinions were never personal opinions, but pronouncements made while in a state of consciousness in which they transcended the finite personality.

In the West we tend to think that if a man is intelligent enough he can know anything. In the East they believe that if he is pure enough he will know everything. They look upon philosophy, the pursuit of knowledge, as a sacrifice to God, and it is one of the paths which lead to Him — the path of *jnana* (knowledge). Until the man has undergone a course of spiritual discipline and self-purification, no truth that he hears will germinate and bear fruit, and he will only be performing lip-service to God by trying to solve His mysteries.

You will now begin to see why the East places such importance on the preliminary yogic training and why they insist on the necessity of being accepted as the pupil of a traditional teacher. The yogic discipline fits the man to obtain that knowledge which leads to union with God, and gives him mastery over all limitations, including death.

Only through purification (and they stress this again and again) will seemingly limited man realize his unlimited and real nature and transform his human consciousness into God-consciousness.

Consciousness does not evolve. It is present in its totality as the substratum of everything all the time, from man to rock, stick or stone, but it is veiled in varying degrees of density. The task of man is to remove these veils, but he cannot do this until he has gained some degree of mastery over his lower nature and recognition of his higher nature. This mastery and understanding is achieved as a result of the yogic training and discipline.

The human mind, dominated by animal instincts, or at best by logic and reason, cannot know God. It operates in the region of duality, and although it may obtain an intellectual conception of Him, it sinks down and evaporates before the vision of non-duality. If the lower mind can only operate in duality, and God is One, how can He be known? Behind the lower mind, so to say, and obscured by the unrest and activity of the lower mind, there is a super-conscious mind, the enlightened intellect — the faculty of spiritual perception — and when the lower mind has been stilled by discipline and the grace and instruction of the teacher, this higher faculty can be located and used.

What are the great questions which every philosophy has to try to solve? Here are four such questions:

1. The nature of God
2. The nature of man and the world
3. The relationship between God and man
4. The goal of life

The primary doctrine of Advaita Vedanta, the sacred science of the East, is unity. It holds that there is one undivided and absolute Consciousness. Man is a part of this Consciousness, this Existence, and the conceptions of love, law, order and universal brotherhood, are indications of the workings of this power of God. It holds that God is all, that God alone is real, that the soul of man and God are intrinsically one, and that the goal of life is to realize this truth — not to know it intellectually but to realize it and be transformed by it.

As has already been said, such tremendous statements will have an awe-inspiring effect on some, while others will consider them to be blasphemous; but do not forget that they have been made by great saints as the result of direct experience, and if you read the testimony of some of the Western mystics and saints with these statements in mind, you will find indications that they too may have had the same experience in their highest state of consciousness, which they only hint at, on account of its unorthodox character.

Now what is meant by the word 'real' in the affirmation 'God alone is real, the world unreal'? The Vedantin uses this word in a special sense. By it he means 'that which is unchangeable, which remains the same through the three categories of time — the past, present and the future', the one subject to which everything conceivable and perceivable is an object. God alone is *That*. He is unchanging Consciousness, Existence which ever was, is now, and ever will be, Bliss absolute, omnipotent and all-pervading.

In this sense, the world and man, who is but an object in the world, are unreal in that they are passing and subject to endless change when judged by the unchanging standards of God. Empirically speaking, however, when looked upon as objects of perception, they are as real as the mind that perceives them. The real meaning of these words will only reveal itself through study, devotion and meditation.

The statement that man is intrinsically God is

open to great misunderstanding, yet it must be made, for it is the cornerstone on which Advaita Vedanta is based. If we wish to consider it, let us purify ourselves and strengthen our super-sensuous faculties so that we may reach a state in which the necessary instruction can be given. 'God alone is real, all else unreal, and God and man are intrinsically one' means that God is all-pervasive, and that no-one, or no thing, can exist apart from Him.

The sages say that everyone must inevitably realize this truth about their divine nature at some time, and perhaps the greatest contribution they have made to the world is that they teach that this knowledge can be obtained in this very life. In fact they affirm that it must be obtained either in this or in some future life on this earth, for it can be obtained nowhere else. This is a startling statement, but one meriting reverent and serious enquiry.

To recognize identity with God, to experience complete liberty — complete fearlessness and bliss — for this all things come into manifestation, gradually evolve from inanimate to animate objects, from manhood to Godhead. According to the holy Adhyatma Yoga, this is the goal of life.

Here finish the indications of the answers to

the four questions set out at the beginning. Now what is their significance when considering man's life as man, on earth?

That Consciousness which binds all things together into one family, so to say, and which is one of the manifestations of God's nature and His power, is seen by the enlightened to operate in this world through law and order. There is, notwithstanding our ignorance and disregard of it, a spiritual law behind the seeming chaos of the world, which the East calls *dharma*. A knowledge and understanding of this law is given by this spiritual Yoga. The results arising from actions performed in obedience to it or in violation of it, are called *karma*. The East believes implicitly in the saying: 'As a man sows, so shall he reap', and this is what is implied by the law of *karma*: the compulsory eating of the fruits of action — of activity, mental, physical, emotional, spiritual.

At this juncture the thought will probably arise in most minds: 'If it is true that there is nothing but God in varying stages of manifestation, why has He created the world at all? Why has He allowed poor man to forget his real divine nature and struggle and suffer?' Just so would a child question if you were to read the scriptures or the *Upanishads* to him: 'Why?' 'What for?' We are all children to the Lord, but we shall grow up in time, and know, not the answers to our questions, but His purpose.

The magic power of the Lord by which He veils Himself and causes unity to appear as diversity is called *maya*. It is the principle of change, and its beauty and significance will only be caught by one whose hearing is pure enough to catch the rhythm of infinity. It is so with all these high truths. They will only reveal themselves to those fitted to receive them. If any feel drawn to make this adventure, they must learn to qualify for instruction. In spiritual experience, problems disappear, for what a man knows, that he becomes. To *know* is to *be*.

VI

PATHS TO ENLIGHTENMENT

THE THREE PATHS! Three steepish paths leading out of that magic wood — the world, and it is surely encouraging to know that the spiritual explorer is not expected to use one royal road only. There is but one royal *end* to this endeavour, and every man will one day inevitably reach it, but not one royal road, for every traveller has his own particular problems, and therefore there are three charted traditional paths by which he can travel, and also many variants of them, perhaps as many as there are applicants for the teachings.

Variety is one of the laws and beauties of nature, and just as the wind draws different notes from every tree — the voice of the open sea from the pine and the sound of the spray from the whitebeam — so at first the Truth evokes different responses from every seeker, and it adds to the interest of the climb that this should be so. But there is an old Japanese verse which reads:

Many paths there be
To reach the mountain's height,

But all who climb there see
The same Moon's light.

Variety may enrich the way, but the goal is oneness — infinity.

Some years ago an enquirer into this Yoga said with an amused smile: 'Well, I don't suppose those old teachers ever came up against anyone like *me*, did they?' Well, he was wrong there, and on at least two counts. First, we may safely deduce from the various ways in which the central teaching from which we obtain our guidance has been transmitted, that the pupils in the olden times must have borne a strong family resemblance to the enquirers of today. The basic passions and needs which control the human mind and heart — and it is better to use the Sanskrit word *antahkarana* here, meaning 'inner organ', because it includes both mind and heart — these needs have not changed very much over the ages.

Which would you say was the desire or basic need which heads all other psychological necessities in man? I don't know what the psychologists of today may have decided, but it seems likely that a 'desire for recognition' comes very high on the list, for it is to be found in varying degrees of virulence in nearly all desires. It masquerades under the mangled name of love, it is nearly always the motive power in ambition, and philanthropy is often its second name. This desire for recognition, usually known as egoity, because it springs from it, is the most insidious of all desires, for it is based, according to the yogic psychology, on a fundamental truth — it springs from man's unconscious acceptance and appreciation of the fact of the presence within him of higher qualities and powers than those he manifests to the world today. Deep within him he harbours the certainty that, given an opportunity, he could justify his existence and demonstrate unsuspected things and also experience a sense of fulfilment by so doing.

This desire for expansion, for self-justification, which man usually places high on his list of demands from life, will, so he thinks, only be fulfilled when he is able to bring about the outer circumstances in which he can reveal *that* which he obscurely feels lies hidden within him, and demonstrate its powers. Of course he seldom visualizes this hidden force as spiritual; usually he envisages it as very much the reverse, but intimations of its existence are present, and as a disturbing factor, in every *antahkarana*. In some it manifests as a driving discontent with restriction; in others, as the presence of a standard of perfection which cannot be achieved; and it makes itself felt in many other and less obvious ways as well.

All desires and inner demands, which are always demands for satisfaction in some form or another, spring from a limited and distorted concept of this hidden yet semi-revealed power. For Yoga teaches that man does recognize, though only dimly and in a distorted fashion, the state of transcendence which will ultimately be his. Not only that — he has sensed it from the beginning of his journey through his incarnations, and this limited concept must ultimately be brought to the surface of consciousness and known for what it is: an intimation of immortality, of perfection.

It may sound a very arbitrary pronouncement to state that man's reactions and his characteristics are influenced by the friction set up between what he guesses to be within himself, and what he receives from the hands of life and his own limitations, but it is the traditional teaching. It is not meant that every man is making straight for the state of spiritual freedom and transcendence all the time, but it does mean that he constantly feels a necessity to expand in some direction, and the impulse to explore his capacities, and reveal and enjoy them. But as we know, when he has brought the first experiment to a successful conclusion, he will again feel thwarted and restricted and will begin another search, and so it will go on until he reaches the state of changeless satisfaction.

Yet, it will be noticed that when facing fresh opportunities for gaining knowledge, and therefore presumably greater scope and power, the mind instinctively starts to limit that opportunity, by turning it into what may be called 'an avenue of approach' only. Minds cannot usually expand or grasp new ideas or wider horizons quickly or easily, so any fresh discovery has to be made manageable, so to say, before it can be accepted. This means that certain aspects of it will be eliminated altogether, while others will be brought into prominence, and this will result in the production of something quite other than the original proposition. In other words, a concept will have been formed, which is easy of acceptance, limited and therefore within the normal psychological range of the *antahkarana*.

A concept is valuable in many ways, but it is also a dangerous thing, for it must necessarily be a travesty of that from which it springs and, far more important, it will always bear the stamp of personal bias — of egoity. It may work satisfactorily and for a long time, provided that nothing occurs to demonstrate its limitations, but eventually inner growth, renewed enquiry and increasing demands will reveal its inadequacy. For instance, electricity is one of the most powerful forces as yet recognized by man, yet when envisaged solely as the producer of warmth, light and energy, it will appear to compress itself into that rôle for a while. Then one day it brings sudden death to the one who is ignorant of its terrific and hidden powers and tampers with them. The dangers attending inadequate knowledge provide the reason why the yogic teachers prize the quality of *vichara*, or detached and constructive enquiry, so highly in their pupils. It keeps them open to fresh discoveries and causes them to discard concept after concept in search of Truth.

There is an old Chinese legend which is not very serious but shows a nice recognition of the danger lurking in concepts. There was once an old sage — at least he wasn't an old sage at all, he turned out to be an old self-deluded man. One day he found a large and convenient cave in a very lonely part of the country and took possession of it, barring the entrance against intruders. He settled in, and the poor country people of the district, who were very charitable *and* credulous, which is not unknown in the East, soon spread the good news that their district had received a special blessing from the Lord because a very holy man had taken up his abode with them. Day by day they trudged up to the cave, calling on him to come out and receive their gifts of food and clothing, and asking for his blessing and the sight of his holy person. But as they approached, they could hear a voice calling from within: 'Begone, O fools! This is holy ground! I am communing with the Dragon and cannot be disturbed by such as you!'

Now, according to Chinese symbology, the dragon is a most awe-inspiring creature, the symbol of immortality, one who would never waste his time on any but the very highest. So the gifts were doubled and many prayers were uttered outside the cave, and they were now addressed to the dragon asking for his protection and permission to serve his devotee. Then one day, as the villagers were working in the open air and singing their songs, they suddenly heard terrible and piercing screams issuing from the cave, and they saw their holy man emerge, running like a hare and pursued by the most terrible, unbelievable, fire-snorting dragon imaginable, definitely not the sort of apparition who would sit in a cave communing with anyone! What could have happened to their holy man? Well, one glimpse of the reality behind his theoretical conception of dragons had been sufficient to reduce him to a moral and spiritual bankrupt, fleeing from the wrath to come. He had realized, too late, that he had not been sitting and communing with a real dragon at all but with a dragon concept — a most dangerous practice! Probably the villagers were not so shattered as he was, probably they went quietly down on their faces, full of veneration, and waited for the pair to disappear in the distance, for they, at any rate, had no preconceived idea or concept of dragons to be demolished.

In the spiritual training there must of necessity be an inwardly held vision of the object of worship, or of the desired culmination of that worship, but it must be recognized for what it is, a changing and expanding concept, an indication of the present spiritual state of the maturing seeker, and therefore liable to change.

But to return on our tracks. We have suggested that probably men have been actuated by very much the same motives throughout the ages, but that these motives, whether high or low, are brought to the surface of consciousness in disguise and robbed of any indication of their original nature. The only example which was given in support of this was the desire for recognition, which, it was contended, springs from a deep yet subconscious sense of greatness, or as the Yoga would say, of Godhead! Only by relinquishing the limited concept of that supreme condition, that is, only by transcending it, can it be realized for what it is, and it was said that Yoga was the means of purifying or simplifying the *antahkarana* in order that this underlying knowledge of Reality could take the place of the ego-tinted concept.

Our teacher once said that it was useless to rely on individual practices for release; and that meditation, mind control, study of the scriptures and physical exercises would have no permanent effect where the egoity or *ahankara*, as it is called, operates unrecognized and unchecked, and that where this is so, the yogic practices will only provide the *ahankara* with secret food. The first function of the practices is to destroy this domination by the ego, and there are tested and traditional ways by which the Gurus teach their disciples how to bring this about.

The concept of the Yoga held by however excellent a pupil, can never be as great as the Yoga in fact is. Some see it as a series of exercises in control; others hope that it will provide occult knowledge whereby they can pass from one plane of consciousness to another; whilst to others it represents a miner's operation to quarry out hidden gold. But according to the teachings of Adhyatma Yoga, this science cannot be confined to any of these categories, for it is the way of inner purification or simplification, as a result of which *that* which through many incarnations has hidden itself in concepts, may reveal its basic reality.

But this talk was not to be about concepts, it should have been about the paths to enlightenment — so let us quickly start! According to the tradition, there are three main ways of arriving at the state of transcendence or beatitude; but let it be said at once that these paths are merely three different methods by which one supreme and life-giving quality may be uncovered and consciously known and practised by man, and particularly by three main types of men. These three classes are the intellectual, the contemplative and the active, and the paths are those of knowledge, of aspiration or devotion, and of action. And what is the supreme and liberating quality, which runs like a clear stream by the side of each path for the preservation of the life of those who walk it? It goes by the name of *identification*, or pre-occupation with the intimations of Reality, and it is produced by inner concentration on a focus. As the gaze intensifies, the nature or qualities of that focus pervade the *antahkarana* of the worshipper and expansion of his concept of this focus takes place.

There is an erroneous idea that these paths vary in their spiritual importance, that those who follow the path of knowledge, for instance, are more spiritually gifted than the followers of the paths of aspiration and action. This is based on a misconception of that part of the teaching which is concerned with the significance of action itself, inner and outer. It is subtle and far-reaching, and it shows that not only on one path, but on every path, thought, which produces all action, outer or inner, should be regarded as part of a continuous offering to the supreme Reality or God — an attitude which serves to establish an unbroken communication between the omnipresent and divine Spirit and man. It is this practice of dedication which matures the pupil whatever his path. After all, there is only one eternal resting place, the Self, the supreme Spirit in man. All else, even the most apparently elevated activities, mental or spiritual, are merely methods of climbing towards it.

So these climbing paths have only one significance. It is to lead the traveller to the end of the journey and, as is the way with mountain tracks, they will take him through more and more exposed country as he approaches the crest. Any one of these paths can lead him to it, provided he uses it as a means to that end, not as a loitering ground which offers attractions of its own to detain him. This is by no means unlikely. The path of knowledge *can* detain the traveller by virtue of the rare mental experiences to be encountered upon it. The path of devotion may confuse him, for there are many tracks leading downwards from it to the den of egoity. The path of service can easily be lost in personal and not dedicated activity, in which case it becomes theoretical service only and not a path. But provided that the path chosen is walked untiringly and with intelligence, it will lead the climber to his desired goal.

To define once again the quality which can lead a climber to his desired end. It is what the world calls devotion but what Yoga calls identification, the pre-occupation with the intimations of perfection, the inner activity through which he will reach that state of consciousness where he knows unity and universality directly. Where it is present, the climb will be invested with life; where absent, or present in a theoretical sense only, the efforts of the climber will be meaningless, a series of gestures in slow motion such as are sometimes seen on a cinema screen. Theoretical knowledge, theoretical devotion — and there is such a thing — and theoretical service are all dead activities, mere mental gymnastics. Theoretical knowledge may be useful at the beginning of the training in order to amass data, but it is not alive, nor can it ever give life to the one who so uses it, that is, it will never make saints or illumined men.

In one of the Eastern classics, the *Ramayana*, which tells the story of the life of the divine incarnation, Shri Rama, there is a good example of the way in which the desire for identification through concentration on a focus can interpenetrate a disciple and turn him into a saint of God. Shri Rama had a disciple, Hanuman, an untutored barbarian depicted in the classics as a monkey. He was simple and his mind was one-pointed, for it was forever contemplating his focus, his teacher

Shri Rama. Shri Rama used to enjoy asking him questions about his spiritual state because the answers he gave were so instantaneous and truthful. This was a disciple who had immersed himself in the real and traditional contemplation — I say real and traditional contemplation because its focus pervaded all the levels of his inner being and governed his actions also.

One day as they sat together, Shri Rama said to him: 'O Hanuman! Tell me, what is thy assured conviction about me and thee?' Hanuman replied at once: 'O Lord, when I think of myself as a body, I am Thy serving slave. When I think of myself as an individual soul, I am Thy fragment — a spark of Thy fire. And when I think of my real nature, O, then I know that I am even as Thou art'. The holy Hanuman was a magician, like all true lovers, for he could walk on all three paths at once. He could, by a turn of his mind, transform himself into a servant, a devotee or a knower, and on whichever path he found himself, and wherever he fixed his attention, he experienced direct contact with the Lord at that point.

But you may say, 'Well, this may be so, but how was it brought about? You say that Yoga is the method whereby a personal concept is expanded into knowledge, and whereby devotion or pre-occupation is produced. How is it done?' Friends, it is done by degrees and by slow and patient climbing. Our teacher used to say that this faculty for devotion is an art and should be learnt and approached as you approach an art. He also said that there were three rising stages by which the disciple learns this art. During the initial stage he is trained to meditate on the fact: *I am His*. His desire is to serve, and he places his reasoning mind and his body at the disposal of his focus, which means that he learns to perform all action as an offering, not as an activity. In the second stage, he is taught to visualize his contact with this focus and to meditate on the fact: *I am Thine*. This is a much nearer relationship than that of a servant and this practice, in the end, turns him into a lover, a devotee. The third stage is the culmination of knowledge. Here the disciple does not meditate, he does not make any affirmation, he knows. What does he know? *I am He*. This is identification and the end of the climb. Each of these successive affirmations or recognitions marks a stage in the transformation of the limited ego into the universal Self, a stage in the transformation of the old concepts into a vision of the basic Truth.

You may say, 'But why must devotion be the

only quality which can effect this change?' In the Yoga the word devotion does not mean emotion. What is meant by devotion is the longing, the flight, towards identification with the supreme Spirit or a manifestation of it. It is brought about by discipline, the sense of conscious direction — which is only another name for dedication — and later on, by prolonged meditation. Each of these practices is given by the teacher in order to free his disciple from his bonds. Every spiritual school has had to stand up to the charge of wanton asceticism, needless restrictions and the arbitrary breaking down of the individual will. But perhaps it will be seen, from what has been indicated in this chapter, that these restrictions are but temporary, although they are necessary, and when undertaken in a traditional school of training, they are undertaken for the purpose of expansion and ultimate identification only.

VII

YOGA IN ACTION

This is a short, simple and, I hope, practical paper on the subject of action. Yoga has been defined as conscious living — the wise performance of action. So it is vital that we shall at least be acquainted with the technique.

Actions are the outer manifestations of an inner activity. They are the effects of a cause, and, as such, they take on the qualities of that cause; if the cause is pure, the effect, or action, is pure, and *vice versa*. Our actions govern our future, perhaps one should say 'the future', for according to the spiritual law of *dharma* — the law of universality of consciousness and basic righteousness — the effects of an action are not confined to the doer.

Most people feel satisfaction when active, and are either conscious-stricken or actively uncomfortable when they are what is known as 'doing nothing'. We may *say* that we long to do nothing, but do we, I wonder? Perhaps all we long for is time to decide what kind of activity we think we are entitled to engage in — next! A mere wish to abandon action is futile; it will not alter the tendencies of the senses, and it is most unwise to try to suppress action, or anything else, by force. It only gives the thing an added reality. The *Bhagavad Gita* calls those who try to do this 'hypocrites':

> He who restrains his organs of action, but continues, in his mind, to brood on the objects of sense, is said to be a hypocrite, O Arjuna. But he who controls the senses by the mind and, without attachment, engages his organs of action in works, he is a superior man. (III.6-7)

This is the verdict of the *Bhagavad Gita*. But there is a notion among what are known as 'practical people' that, as a man ascends in the spiritual scale, he becomes more and more aristocratic, so to say, and his action decreases, until, when he reaches his goal, a state ensues where activity ceases altogether. This is one of the reasons why saints are at a discount today, when activity and competition are in the air, but one has only to look at the example of the sages and saints, both past and present, to see what an erroneous idea this is.

One thinks of Shri Shankaracharya, who only lived for thirty years, but who poured out commentaries and works of the highest philosophical importance, founding monasteries in the north, south, east and west of India, a God-realized sage, a poet and a Guru; of St Teresa, writing, organizing, training her nuns, working without ceasing; of St Francis, St Bernard — their numbers will, please God, never cease. They were volcanoes of power, always in a state of enlightened and compassionate eruption, but the source from which their power was drawn was of the Spirit. It emanated from a region other than their physical and mental bodies, for they had established a fusion with that source, and were its instruments. The practical man is also a volcano of power, but his power has its origin in his mind and emotions, and to it he is often a slave.

In both cases the energy which is generated is translated into action; but one will be effortless, gratuitous, and carried out with what has been called 'divine recklessness', while the other will be accompanied by tension, effort, blood and tears — effort and tension, the hallmark of the novice! The old Chinese philosopher Chuang Tzu has said:

> Those whose hearts are in a state of repose give forth a divine radiance, by the light of which they see themselves as they are. Only by cultivating such repose can a man attain the constant. Those who are

constant are sought after by men and assisted by God.

The activity of the saints and sages is endless and concentrated, but it is also subtle and hidden. The duties of their calling (whatever that may be) even their walking, talking, eating and breathing, are a prayer and a call to worship; whereas the unenlightened man fluctuates between intense effort and an inertia which is productive of nothing except perhaps some physical energy with which he can press on again.

As has already been said, effortlessness is the hallmark of the adept, tension of the novice. Therefore, once a man has started on the spiritual quest, any hope placed on mere effort is misplaced. The less force used on the mind and body, the better. Relaxation promotes circulation, and unimpeded circulation is as much a necessity for the mind and emotions as it is for the body; consequently, actions will suffer and become distorted, and even gangrenous, where there has been tension and restriction in the mind and emotions from which they spring.

But even effortless action will not lead directly to the goal; it is only a means to that end and a means of clearing the way to attainment. At this point, the pseudo-critic, by whom I mean one who is after flaws and not truth, will make the statement that if action of itself is incapable of producing enlightenment, it obviously is meant to be given up and therefore the Yoga stands revealed as the science of escapism. Q.E.D.

This is not so. Action is not decried in any of the spiritual classics of this philosophy. There is indeed an old legend of India which teaches very clearly the importance attached to action. It is told that at the beginning of time, the Lord had seven sons, born of His own mind. When they were introduced into the world, they refused to take any part in the drama and sat in contemplation, neither begetting sons nor works. Was the Lord satisfied with such an attitude? No. He pronounced Himself dissatisfied, and He created the great Sages, Shri Vasishtha and many others, who took wives, and lived lives of cosmic and earthly value.

It is only when action is used by man as a vehicle for his own personal desires and aversions, or as a mere release for his surplus energy, that the warning is given.

The Adhyatma Yoga has for its scripture the *Bhagavad Gita* and there is no spiritual classic in the world in which the psychology of action has been more exhaustively and subtly examined. The immediate situation which gave rise to the teachings being given was the failure of Prince Arjuna to understand the true meaning of action. The classic opens on a field of battle, and the contest is between two branches of the same family. The Lord of the Universe, the divine Incarnation Shri Krishna, has undertaken to guide the chariot of Prince Arjuna on the field.

The Prince is of the *Kshatriya* caste, a warrior, one to whom action is natural and right. Up to the beginning of the story, his warlike activities have been carried out as a duty to his caste, as his contribution to the community, and they have been uncoloured by any emotion — in fact they have been rightly conceived actions. Now his opponents are of his own blood, and he suddenly feels himself identified and emotionally involved with the results of his actions and therefore determines to avoid the issue and not to fight.

He turns to the Lord and tells Him he wishes to become a monk, asks Him to accept him as a disciple and to instruct him in his duty, having, after the immemorial manner of pupils, stated what he is and what he is *not* prepared to do. Then the Lord, gently smiling on his youth and rawness, accepts him as His, and begins to teach. That teaching is the *Bhagavad Gita*.

One would think that the Lord would launch at once into a discourse on action and duty, personal and communal, but Shri Krishna does not do so. First he reveals to his pupil the highest secret, the goal of all endeavour, the supreme Truth of the deathless Self and man's identity with it. In other words, he first gives Arjuna a glimpse of the limitless background, to lift his heart, before he discourses on the well-known foreground. It is always so with the true teachers; they transmute their pupils by changing their sense of values, not by a logical statement of the *pros* and *cons* of an immediate situation.

Thus, it is only after having shown him the goal, that Shri Krishna begins to give the teachings on the steps that lead to that goal.

We too can only learn how to act rightly if at the outset we grasp the true motives for action: worship of the Lord through His creation and our powers, and obedience to Him by keeping His laws in action. Love and obedience — the pure incentives to action.

Now to go into detail. Action may be grouped under three heads:

1. Automatic action or *re*action. Dr Shastri did not call this action; he called it activity.
2. Actions emanating from the reason, emotions

and egoity, which are done in response to conscious or unconscious motives and impulses.
3. Actions done when in conjunction with the supra-mental or higher Power; inspired or enlightened action.

The first category, automatic activity, contains those reactions which are called forth by the instincts, and to which no impetus is given by the intelligence. The acts of eating, sleeping, avoiding danger, are examples of this category. These activities are common both to men and animals. They are not subject to change, they are harmless, inasmuch as they carry no *karma* or results. If you say: 'O yes they do. Eating — indigestion!' the meaning of eating here is the automatic reaction to hunger, and not the sitting-down-and-choosing-something-to-enjoy kind of eating.

The actions in the second category are inspired by emotions good and bad, by desire and by egoity. They are generally carried out with a definite purpose, namely that they shall have a successful issue or fruit. If the doer is a beginner (as most of us are), he identifies himself, through ignorance and insufficiency of discipline, with these results, and he suffers or enjoys, as they appear to him to be successful or unsuccessful.

The third category is that of enlightened

actions done in conjunction with the supra-mental power. No one can act systematically according to the rules governing this category until he has passed through a period of instruction, purification and discipline, and has come out at the other end; but once he has decided to persist in this training and to come out at the other end, his entry into this category of action is only a question of time, patience and continuity of purpose.

Here the man does not stretch his imagination forward towards results of any action, for he now realizes that he cannot know the cosmic purpose with his finite mind, nor indeed what is ultimately desirable or undesirable; so he places his body, mind and emotions as instruments in the hands of the Lord to be used for His purposes. He does not go about seeking opportunities for action, but, in the words of the *Gita*:

> Satisfied with what comes to him unsought, though acting, he is not bound.... In this world he has no interest whatever to gain by actions he has done, and none to gain by the actions he has not done. Nor does he depend on any being for any object. (IV.22, III.18)

Such is the man of enlightened action. Later he passes beyond all categories, and becomes unpredictable, a law unto himself, because his self is now one with the One.

In a certain sense, the first and third categories have points in common. Both are automatic; perhaps it would be nearer the mark to say one is automatic and the other spontaneous, but in one the source of the stimulus comes from the individual centre and in the other from the Point of God. In fact the third category might be said to be a harmonic of the first.

It is with the second category, however, that we are now concerned, for all action, as we know it at present, comes within its scope. Dr Shastri has said that first we must be good, then godly, then divine and then perfect, even as our Father in Heaven is perfect. The progress from good to godly action takes place in the second category. Divine action — not action which is divine, but action which emanates from a higher source — is reserved for the third category, while perfection belongs to no category at all.

One of the dangers of making categories is that an illusion of tidiness, manageability and inevitability is created, whereas in fact the lines of demarcation between categories are often very faint. For instance, although within the category with which we are dealing — the second — the motives for action will always spring from the personal centre, that centre may be pure or turgid. The actor may be a man of great spiritual experience, or he may be a beginner, struggling in the grip of his motives.

The *Gita*, as we have said, makes it clear that action is inevitable and necessary, and that it is not action which hinders spiritual progress but the idea that you are its instigator, that you are doing it and that you therefore have a proprietary interest in its result.

This attitude gives action an alluring yet dangerous quality; for when you identify yourself with an act and its results, not only do you lay yourself open to the events which it brings in its train, but you violate two central doctrines of the Advaita philosophy upon which this Yoga is based. They are non-identification and the law of *dharma*. Non-identification means the non-identification of the individual with phenomena, mental and physical, and his identification with the Real.

The law of *dharma* is the law which teaches that all life is one, and that man is a link in a vast chain of Consciousness, a chain into which are forged all objects — atoms, rocks, animals, man himself and the higher intelligences. It lays down that man is a microcosmic aspect of the Lord, that his mind is part of the Lord's mind, his body a part of the cosmic body of the Lord and his creative energy a part of the creative energy of the Lord of Creation.

According to this law, man's every thought and action has an influence for good or evil on the rest of the chain and therefore, when his thoughts and actions are selfish, they generate a kind of tension in society which is bound to react on him in due course. Man's mind and body are in reality the servants of the Spirit, and the object of their activity should be to serve the Spirit and to disclose the fact of its reality to all.

Thus, so long as man visualizes himself as an independent unit, and imagines that he, personally, is capable of giving a direction to affairs, and that it is desirable for him to do so, he is going against this universal law. He may be working for what his reason tells him will benefit himself, or (if he has become slightly de-centralized) for what he thinks is good for you, or what at any rate he thinks you ought to have; but in either case he is a danger, for his actions will bring reactions.

This is the stage of development which Chuang Tzu describes when he says: 'Now the well-intentioned start tripping up people with charity and fettering them with duty to their neighbours. What with their gushing over music and fussing over ceremony, the whole empire becomes confused and divided against itself.'

In other words, such a man becomes confused and divided against himself, because the source from which his activity springs is confused, divided and impure. Such is worldly or unenlightened action, however well-intentioned it may be: the class of action that we — each one of us — have spent incarnations performing. Perhaps it has not been a waste of time, for nothing can be permanently and consciously relinquished until it is known for what it is, and it is the disappointing taste of the fruits of such unenlightened action which, in the end, disillusions man and brings him to a spiritual path.

Now he must undergo a training as a result of which action will be robbed of its karmic power. Unenlightened action leads to *karma* good and bad — to the upholding of the world process (*sansara*) — and *karma* leads to endless future births and deaths. Yoga has in view nothing less than the ending or liquidating of *karma*; for, being the science of purified and enlightened action, it leads to the unveiling of that higher wisdom, through knowledge of which, *karma* is arrested and finally brought to a standstill.

Although action may not lead directly to God, the offering of each act and its fruits to Him does. Therefore the teacher in the *Gita* instructs his pupil how to act in such a way that he may not be bound, how to perform action as an actor or agent without the sense of responsibility or doership.

To silence one loud voice and to become sensitive enough to detect the still small voice of Spirit, is now the purpose of the pupil. How is this to be done ? It is done through the traditional training of an authentic Yoga. By learning to awaken devotion in the heart; by listening to the Truth, cogitating on the Truth, and meditating on the Truth, that Truth which began as a surmise, will become a reality.

Devotion is the equanimity of one whose heart rests in the Lord, and it is a mighty power. Works turn into devotion when the heart is so fixed, and only when this transformation has taken place, can the enlightened action of the third category be even envisaged. Once a small degree of success in the training has been attained, however, man begins to free himself from the idea that he is a pocket Creator, and he can even envisage the possibility of acting in a drama which he has not written himself.

When it is said that man should perform action as an actor and not as an initiator, many jump to the conclusion that an irresponsible attitude to life will result. But when we go to a play, we do not expect to see an actor drawling through his part because he is not responsible for the script. On the contrary, we expect him to act with as much intensity as if he had written the part; and so, no doubt, do the audience of mighty Gods expect us to act in their cosmic drama, without adding or leaving out a single line, but with all our might and intelligence. To act as in a drama and to present the reading of our part to the Lord, is enlightened action.

At this point there are some who will say: 'Yes, the more important actions in life may be offered in that way, but not the everyday actions'. There is a poem by Shri Shankaracharya which is called *Mental Worship*. It says:

> O Lord, Thou art my Self. My intellect is Thy consort, my sense organs Thy attendants, this body is Thy temple, ministering to the senses, my act of worship to Thee. My sleep is *samadhi*, my moving about on foot is an act of circumambulation, all the words I speak are hymns to Thee, whatever works I do are Thy worship, O Lord. Glory be to Thee!

Every action and every part is here pressed into the service, so that the mind, having through training convinced itself of its part in the ritual, may subconsciously fulfil it minute by minute. The great Ramanuja Acharya says:

> The cardinal doctrine of the *Gita* is love of God, one-pointed and intense, which asks nothing but the honour and delight of serving Him.

Advaita philosophers might have something to add to this statement, but for our purposes, it is sufficient. 'The honour and delight of serving Him' is a very good definition of the basis of enlightened action.

At this juncture it is reasonable to ask: 'How may one know what is acceptable to the Lord?' The delusion that one can easily know the will of God, is one of the happy hunting grounds of the ego. The voice of God is not easily distinguishable, nor are His orders clear to the unpurified. When I was working for a firm of solicitors, we once had a letter from a client who was an Oxford Groupist*. She said that she regretted very much, but she must take her work away. God had spoken to her in her morning prayers, and had said: 'My child, you must leave that firm.

* Member of a religious sect which flourished in England in the 1930s

They charge too much, the Trust cannot stand it!'

In fact, the state of purity in which the will of God may be known cannot be attained without self-discipline, enquiry and continuity of purpose; for nothing is to be had without paying its price. When the price has been paid, then the pupil is on the way to become an adept. Instantaneous perception, instantaneous reaction and instantaneous forgetting are his characteristics. Actions are presented to him, they are carried out instantaneously and banished at once from his consciousness 'leaving not a wrack behind'. He is joined now to his Source — not one with it (that comes later), but joined to it — and moves preoccupied and identified as a dancer moves through an intricate dance, responsive to the subtle rhythm of the music which he alone can hear.

If you say that this state is not possible to achieve, then the higher teachings of Yoga are not possible, and as they form part of the foundation on which it is built, the whole structure falls to the ground. But it *is* possible, for it has been demonstrated again and again by the saints of every religion. Chuang Tzu has two descriptions of such a man:

> A drunken man who falls out of a cart, though he may suffer, does not die. His bones are the same as

> other people's, but he meets his accident in a different way. His spirit is in a condition of security. He is not conscious of riding in the cart, neither is he conscious of falling out of it. Ideas of life, death and fear cannot penetrate his breast, so he does not suffer from the contact with the objective existence. If such security is to be got out of wine, how much more is it to be got from God. It is in God that the sage seeks his refuge, and so he is free from harm.

The second is:

> The true sage, when in obscurity, causes those around him to forget their poverty; when in power, he causes princes to forget rank and emoluments, and to become as though of low estate. He rejoices exceedingly in all creation. Though silent, he can instil peace and by his mere presence cause men to be to each other as father and son. From his very return to passivity comes this active influence for good. All things are to him as One, yet he knows not that this is so, it is simply nature. In the midst of action he remains the same. He makes God his guide, and men make him theirs. The love of a sage for his fellows finds expression among mankind. Were he not told so, he would not know that he loved his fellows. But whether he knows it or whether he does not know it, whether he hears it or whether he does not hear it, his love for his fellow men is without end, and mankind ceases not to repose therein.

This stage, although high, is not the end of man's journey, but it describes the consummation of enlightened action, as mankind can envisage it.

VIII

THE THREE GUNAS

IT IS generally held that the man of today is pre-eminently a questioner and a researcher, that he *must* have a reason for everything and that he will never be satisfied to take things on trial or on faith.

But from what we can gather from the classics of the East, modern man is beaten out and out by the thinkers of ancient India. There seems however to be a fundamental difference in their attitude towards research. Modern man hopes to arrive at Truth through deduction and reasoning and by refusing to advance further than his mind can see and accept. The ancient thinkers, on the other hand, did not place so much faith or value in reasonable theories, so they did not necessarily discard them when they fell short of logical certainty. They looked on research as moves in the game of unveiling the supreme Truth, moves made in order to keep that Truth, which they had already intuitively accepted, in partial focus, while they trained their higher faculties to grasp it in its entirety.

Thus, although the clarion call of the Advaita

philosophy is 'God alone is real and the world is unreal', there are clearly defined descriptions of the creation and constitution of the world and phenomena, which are considered to be helpful to the student in so far as they give his mind something to rest in while he is preparing himself for a direct vision of the truth of Reality.

To such a category of mental activity belongs the conception of *maya* or *prakriti* and the three *gunas*. *Maya* or *prakriti* is the substance, divine, immaterial, inexplicable, through which all creation, physical and mental, is produced, and the three *gunas* are the inherent characteristics of this substance.

All phenomena are said to be brought into being through a fusion of all-pervading Consciousness with *prakriti* and the three *gunas*, which constitute its triple nature. *Prakriti* is the power through which the Infinite is made to appear as finite and it is thus the power which conceals the nature of Reality. It is a mystery, never seen, but known to exist by virtue of its effects. Through its finitizing quality and its characteristic of constant becoming, it manifests its presence as time and space, as matter, as the body and mind and the emotions — in fact, as all phenomena, mental and physical.

Maya or *prakriti* is thus the power which produces appearances. The world of appearance is its handiwork or effect. The world is therefore not a complete deception or hallucination, but it *is* the occasion for deception, for here the supreme Truth or Reality is veiled and distorted.

Now when we use the word 'veiled', we bring the conception of the *gunas* into the picture. The veiling power of *maya* is supplied by the *gunas*. Reality, Consciousness Absolute, is self-luminous and self-revealing, but it is veiled by the *gunas* or states of density of *maya*. The *gunas* form, so to say, a shifting screen which hides Reality, as clouds veil the light of the sun. They are three in number and cover the three stages from the most complete to the most translucent veiling. Their names and the effect of their individual veiling capacities are:

Tamas. This produces the most complete veiling. It is the obscuring factor, manifesting as the inertness in matter, and error, laziness and absence of discrimination in the mind.

Rajas. This produces a less complete veiling. It is the principle of activity, manifesting as life in all things, and activity, desire, selfishness and greed in the mind.

Sattva. This produces the most tenuous veil. It is the principle of transparency and reflection, manifesting as the inner organ or personality in man and producing in it the qualities of balance, virtue and understanding.

It is difficult to think of a simile which will give any idea of the individual characteristics of the *gunas.* Perhaps the English weather would be the best. *Sattva* would correspond to 'set fair', with quiet atmosphere pervaded by sun — an unusual weather condition, and a most unusual *guna* to be in the ascendant for long. *Rajas* — 'changeable'. Can produce whirlwinds or soft breezes — the most usual type of weather and the most usual *guna* to find in the ascendant in man. And *tamas* — 'deep depression' with attendant secondaries.

Or we might say *tamas* corresponds to the static earth, *rajas* to the volatile moving air and *sattva* to the light which permeates the earth and the air. And here it should be pointed out that the earth is not only to be thought of as a mass of immovable matter, but as the support and basis on which the world structure is built. So is *tamas* a sustaining *guna* in its higher manifestations.

The *gunas* act together, never separately, for

together they form the moving, shifting texture of *maya*, but one or other of them is said to be always in the ascendant. They are all present in matter, mind and life, but in varying degrees of density. Thus although *tamas* predominates in matter, matter also contains (if you can use the word) the *sattva guna*, the principle which reflects or manifests Consciousness most clearly. Therefore Consciousness is not only present, but faintly discernible, in even the lowest forms of matter. Matter is resistant, for it has the *tamas guna* predominating; but although it may appear stable to the eye, every particle is capable of change and motion. In other words, *rajas* is present. There is also rhythm in this movement, indicating the presence of *sattva*. As in matter, so in man. He also is an admixture, all three *gunas* being present in him. Therefore he has no cause for complete hopelessness, or complacency. He will never be safe until he has reached his home, so to say; that is, until the influence of the *gunas* has been neutralized and transcended.

The *gunas* not only consort together, but they may be said to aid each other; for without the presence of *tamas*, *rajas* would destroy itself and *sattva*; without the influence of *rajas*, *tamas* would never move; and without *tamas*, *sattva* might perhaps dissipate into thin air.

At this point one asks oneself, 'Is there any purpose in this perpetual interchange?' According to Vachaspati Mishra, a great philosopher of the tenth century, there *is* a purpose. He says:

> Like a lamp, their action is for a single purpose. The wick and the oil in a lamp are each by themselves opposed to the action of fire, but they co-operate when in contact with fire for the single purpose of giving light. The various humours of the body, though possessed of contradictory properties, co-operate for the single purpose of sustaining the body. In the same manner do the three gunas, though possessed of mutually contradictory properties, co-operate towards a single end — the emancipation of the Spirit.

How does this emancipation take place and why? The true nature of the spirit of man is complete freedom and sovereignty, and he will not be satisfied until he has unveiled his nature and lives in it. He will therefore be impelled at long last to free himself from any domination or restriction whatsoever, and the most complete domination is servitude to the action of the *gunas*. Spiritual training, discipline and instruction has therefore emancipation as its goal, and the progression is from the domination of *tamas* to the ascendancy of *sattva* and then beyond that.

Before saying more about the importance of the action of the *gunas* to the individual, there are a few general points to be made. According to the *Bhagavad Gita*, the effect of the *gunas* permeates and interpenetrates all things, material and subtle; and in chapters seventeen and eighteen, food, speech, action, the intellect and the qualities are all analyzed and divided into their appropriate admixture of *gunas*. The four castes of India, or, as we would call them, the four prevailing types of mankind, are also placed in categories by virtue of the *guna* prevailing in them. In the *brahmins*, or the men of enlightenment, as we would call them, *sattva* is said to be in the ascendant. In the *kshatriyas* or warriors, with us the men of action, *rajas* rules, mixed with *sattva*. In the *vaishyas*, or the merchant class, with us the materialistic section of the community, *rajas* is in the ascendant mixed with *sattva*; while in the *shudra*, or the unevolved human being, *tamas* is mixed with *rajas*.

To go from the general to the particular.

How do the *gunas* affect us? The *gunas* bind, and their bondage lasts even after death. The ascendancy of one *guna* may colour the life and the actions performed during that life. This means that the man in whom *rajas* predominates will find the lonely forest as full of temptations as a city, while the man of *sattva* will be able to live in the midst of the world as on a mountain top.

The veiling of *tamas* hides the light of the Self. Then man is unconscious of his true nature and is in a state of bemusement. *Rajas* allows the light of the Self to appear in flashes. Then man is partially conscious of his nature, but he turns outward for support. *Rajas* is the *guna* of vicarious enjoyment. It enters the fortress of the personality through the loophole of imagination and the eager savouring of the quality of things — what one translator of *The Crest Jewel of Discrimination* calls 'the caressing of the imagination'. *Sattva* produces a fuller consciousness of the Self, and the man now turns inward on his own nature for support. It is the *guna* of pure enjoyment and reflection.

At this point a query arises. It has been said that the *gunas* are in constant movement. It is therefore rather bewildering to hear such phrases as 'the ascendancy of one *guna* colours the life' or 'a *rajasic* man' or 'a *tamasic* action', as if the *rajasic* or *tamasic* were always in the ascendant and there were no oscillation at all. The answer is that just as on an April day you may say 'On the whole it has been a fine day' although there has been rain and wind as well as sun, so within the rhythm of their movement, one *guna* predominates over varying periods of time.

Action and the motives for action being the most important and practical question for the average man, what part do the *gunas* play in action and in the causes of action? The *gunas* provide the cause for action and they also effect the quality of the action when performed. In the third chapter of the *Gita* it is said:

> By non-performance of action, none reaches actionlessness; by merely giving up action no-one attains perfection. (III.4)

An action is the effect of a cause, and the motive for action lies in the *guna* under which it is carried out. This verse makes it clear that so long as a man busies himself with controlling the effect and ignoring the cause, he runs the risk of being called a hypocrite, as he is elsewhere in the *Gita*, and is fighting a losing battle. The *sattva guna* must be in the ascendant before renunciation can bear fruit. In an old classic there is this pronouncement on such conduct:

> Fools deceived by *maya* and the *gunas* hope to attain liberation by eating one meal a day, by fasting and other acts which enervate the body. What liberation can such ignorant ones get by torture of the body? Donkeys go about naked; are they therefore yogis? Deer and other animals live on grass, leaves and water; are they therefore yogis? All such practices deceive. The only direct cause of liberation is knowledge of the Truth, and the world is the seat of liberation.

There is much instruction in the *Gita* on how to transcend the *gunas* and so control action and conserve energy, and we will return to this in a moment; but there is also a verse on the performance of action which is interesting. It says:

> The *gunas* of *prakriti* perform all action. With understanding deluded, the ignorant man thinks 'I am the doer'. (III.27)

This verse is sometimes tortured into 'I am not responsible for my actions for it is the *gunas* that are acting'. But nothing in this world is ever so easy as that! We *are* responsible in so far that we offer the suitable soil in which a specific *guna* can flourish and action can germinate and then bear fruit. Yet in this verse the true position is implied. It is the attraction of the *gunas* for each other that causes reaction and therefore action. They cause the reaction in the subtle senses and the responses thereto in the gross body. The true Self is detached from the senses, the mind, and — in the end — from the *gunas* as well; but only when this fact is a direct experience and has therefore become an ever-present certainty, acted upon automatically, has the man earned the right to dissociate himself from his reactions and actions. By that time the false self will have dissipated in the light of the true Self, and the man will have become as incapable of doing harm as a snake with its poison fangs removed.

Now about the imprisoning and action-producing power of the *gunas*. There are some verses in the *Gita* which say:

> *Sattva, rajas* and *tamas*: these *gunas*, born of *prakriti*, bind fast in the body the Indestructible, the embodied One. Now *sattva* prevails, having overpowered *rajas* and *tamas*; now *rajas*, having

> overpowered *sattva* and *tamas*; now *tamas*, having overpowered *sattva* and *rajas*. *Sattva* binds all to happiness, knowledge and virtue; *rajas* binds by attachment to action, causing desire and greed; and *tamas* by attachment to sloth, resistance and heedlessness. (XIV.5-8, 10)

Perhaps, after all, one should not use the word 'bind'. Perhaps, dear Brutus, the fault lies not in our *gunas*, but in ourselves that we are underlings! For the *guna* that plays havoc with your and my peace of mind can never disturb or entrap an enlightened man. Why? Because there is no desire or false identification in him for it to adhere to, so to say. The liberated man can look on the perpetual oscillation of the *gunas* as a detached spectator. He can watch them destroy each other's effects and be themselves destroyed like waves of the sea, and, like waves of the sea, rise into activity once more. The purpose of the practices and discipline of the spiritual schools is to teach the disciple how he may, Christ-like, walk on those waves and still their tumult.

It is now time to consider how a man may free himself from the domination of the *gunas* and attain an altitude from where he can enjoy them, yet remain untouched by them.

There is an Eastern saying, 'While the pearl

is still in the oyster, it cannot decorate the royal crown'. So long as we are netted down and in thrall to anything, our true nature is hidden from us and we are in bondage. Balance, so long as it is consciously maintained, contains within it the seed of the fear of falling. It needs courage to maintain a balance, but fearlessness comes when both feet are on the ground, from an inability to perceive duality anywhere.

The various aspects of the training: *meditation*, which is the emptying of the heart of temporal concepts in order to fill it with the infinite and abstract; *control of the mind*, which involves controlling the *cause* of its activity and not the activity itself; and *concentration*, which is the sustaining of the *sattva guna* — all these practices involve an attempt to rise above the cause of ignorance: the *gunas*. Actions, mental and physical, are only the effects of the *gunas*. Therefore discipline and training first aim at a partial control of the *gunas* and then at transcending their influence. They are to be rendered sterile of effect, that is to say, robbed of their quality of cause, and recognized as subtle appearances only; then they will have no power to harm.

The influence of the *gunas* over man can only

be broken when the transcendence of something greater than they has been recognized and acknowledged. The Lord in the *Gita* says:

> Verily this divine illusion of Mine, made up of the *gunas*, is hard to surmount. Only those who devote themselves to Me alone cross over it. (VII.14)

The last *guna* to be surmounted, as you will guess, is the *sattva guna*, and the ancient *rishis* called this process 'the leap in the dark'. You often hear students say that the *sattva guna* has to be transcended, which always sounds slightly patronising to me considering how little of that *guna* is to be found in the average personality; but the old writer Jnaneshvara gives a reason for this which is understandable. He says:

> He who knows his perfection cannot have any lustre added to him by *sattva*, any more than the ocean can increase in volume by receiving the drops of rain.

And when the pupil, Prince Arjuna, asks his teacher in the *Gita*, 'What are the marks of a man who has passed beyond the *gunas*?', he is told, in effect, that such a man watches their activity as a spectator, having now nothing to gain from them. The *gunas* stage a very fine show, but it is meant to be played before an audience of liberated beings.

Now to sum up what has been said: *Maya* or *prakriti* is the inexplicable power through which all creation, gross and subtle, is produced. The three *gunas* are inherent characteristics of that power. They are not concrete, although, in order to deal with them at all, one has to speak as though they were. One says: '*Rajas* does this', or '*Sattva* produces that'. This is not a correct way of speaking — it is only convenient. The *gunas* are not qualities of *prakriti* or *maya,* but they *are* the cause of qualities and states, both in mind and matter. They interpenetrate everything from the universal to the individual. As a result of their interaction, concrete objects take on their characteristics, and man, his mental atmosphere, so to say.

The *gunas* continually play or interact and they will continue to do so, so long as *sansara*, or the world, continues to be. But man has in him the power to rise above the realm of *maya*, or *sansara*, and live in the realm of eternal light, of which he is the Sun, just as it is now possible for him to rise through the belt of alternating atmospheric conditions round the earth into the still stratosphere.

The sage sees the perpetual movement of the *gunas*, but he does not take it seriously; he does not give it any importance. If you give a thing importance, you give it reality and the sage gives reality to nothing save his own Self (*Atman*). Nevertheless he probably enjoys the play of the *gunas*. To a strong swimmer an angry sea is an exhilaration and a joy; to the beginner it is a terror and a danger also. The strong swimmer knows he can reach the shore at will, but the beginner has no time to think of the shore, so busy is he battling with the buffeting waves.

When we have been considering some aspect of *maya*, Dr Shastri tells us we should always end by re-affirming the Advaita position. Here it is: Through the power and fact of *Brahman*, or the Supreme, all appearance, spiritual, mental and physical, comes into temporary manifestation. There is, in effect, nothing intrinsically real but pure *Brahman*; all else is name and form. The changing, shifting *gunas* enrich the shadow show, but have no more permanent reality than the shadow itself. The liberated man lives in the full shadowless light of Reality.

Here is a description of such a man given by a great modern sage, Swami Mangalnathji:

That great hero shines in his high pre-eminence. He is wise. He has attained the state of non-duality. He has gone beyond all duties, and is most peaceful, being free from all desires. He has thrown away all his fighting weapons. He has nothing more to do with any qualifications and therefore, relinquishing all in his Self (*Atman*), that hero enjoys his endless glory, resting in Himself. When that blessed Lord, who Himself has entered the unreal body with its veins and arteries, knows his own nature, there is nothing that can resist him.*

* from *The Triumph of a Hero (Vira Vijaya)* translated by Hari Prasad Shastri, published by Shanti Sadan.

IX

HOW TO SUCCEED IN YOGA

MAN IS born into this world for one purpose only, that is to know God. The process by which he comes to this knowledge, the preliminary purification, the study and the training generally, is called Yoga, There is but one God, but as many Yogas as there are true ways of reaching Him.

In the holy and ancient Adhyatma Yoga there are three ways of approach to the goal, paths within the Path so to say, and these are:

1. The path of knowledge
2. The path of enlightened action—service
3. The path of devotion

There are also three preliminary qualifications which must be present in some degree before progress can be made in Yoga, or in any study worthy of the name. These three qualifications are:

1. Desire and reverence for the knowledge sought — and here the word 'knowledge' is used in the sense of mental and spiritual illumination.

2. Willingness to make the necessary sacrifices to acquire that knowledge.

3. Confidence in the one chosen to impart that knowledge.

Desire and reverence for the knowledge sought can only be generated by association with those who have already given themselves to the search for Truth, and study of the classics. Association with the good and study! Study does not merely mean hearing or reading, but enquiry, and brooding upon the subject, until the mind and heart expand in reverence before the glory and truth revealed to them. This practice entitles the candidate to enter upon the path of knowledge.

The second qualification is willingness to make the necessary sacrifices to acquire knowledge. What does this entail? In this school of thought, it is taught that the body and mind are instruments to be used and governed by the Spirit, or higher Consciousness in man. The ordinary man, before the first premonitions of true knowledge come to him, is an instinctive, unconscious being. Through instruction, he becomes Self-conscious, and stands free and apart from his instruments, using them according to the dictates of the higher knowledge, which is his by nature.

Therefore, the body, mind and heart have to be controlled, and when controlled, bent to the purpose of the Spirit. This process is called 'purification', and courage, patience and enthusiasm are required to carry it through.

What is 'impurity'? The prime cause of impurity is the conviction of separateness, leading, as it does, to selfish action, selfish ends, vanity, desire for power and so on. So long as man has the conviction that he is doing good, or being good, or that he has the power, through his mind or reason, to know what is good, he is impure and, from the higher point of view, a menace to himself and others. It is only after man has pulled down the barriers of personality, which he has erected through many incarnations between himself and his fellow men, and has realized that he and they are one in essence and grounded in divine Consciousness, and has lifted up his heart, mind and senses and offered them to God, that he becomes a channel through which the eternal river of grace can flow.

This purification of his instrument leads man on to the path of enlightened action—service, the second of the three aspects, or approaches, in the Adhyatma Yoga.

How is this purification to be accomplished, or at any rate well started? The *Bhagavad Gita* teaches that every action, every thought and every emotion should be looked upon as a sacrifice, an offering to God, and that if this attitude is adopted and maintained, man will loose himself from the binding and dangerous sense that he is the doer and will overcome attachment to the result of his actions, which are two of the prime causes of impurity. According to the *Gita,* it is not by ceasing to act, or to love, or to learn, that man becomes universalized, balanced and harmless to himself and others, but it is by dedicating every action, every love and every thought, and their fruits, to God, who will then use them for His own, very often inscrutable, purposes — that man can escape from the servitude of self-imposed limitations, and become free.

In the *Bhagavad Gita,* the Lord says:

> Perform thy duties in a spirit of detached devotion to God, unaffected by success or failure. Yoga is inner equilibrium. The world is bound by action, unless performed for the sake of sacrifice. Whatever thou doest, whatever thou eatest, whatever thou givest, do it as an offering to Me. Thus shalt

thou be liberated from the bonds of action and shalt come to Me. (II.48, III.9 & IX.27-28)

Harmlessness in thought, word and deed, disinterested action, equilibrium of the mind and heart, are all possible where every thought and action is started and concluded as a sacrifice, an offering to God. Meditation, prayer and ruthless self-examination are necessary to achieve this state, and to bring the candidate to this great transformation of heart and mind, a teacher is necessary; which brings us to the third qualification, confidence in the one chosen to impart the knowledge.

People say 'When the pupil is ready the teacher arrives', 'Seek and ye shall find; knock and it shall be opened to you'; but what do 'readiness', 'seeking' and 'knocking' imply? They imply that a great decision has been taken which has permeated behind the mind into the innermost being of man, that the will has directed the eyes henceforward to search the horizon and not to gaze about and satiate the senses with sights, that the will has ordered the hand to knock, and not to grasp or strike any more — in a word, that man has begun to use his instruments with a purpose and to an end.

When this stage is reached, the senses, heart

and mind of the man are sufficiently purified to enable him to recognize spiritual eminence, and to reverence and follow it when he encounters it, as he assuredly will.

When recognition and reverence are awake in the heart, it is not so very difficult to arouse the obedience, courage and continuity of purpose necessary to transform the candidate into a true pupil.

This effort leads him on to the third approach to the Yoga, the path of devotion, for it is through his reverence and devotion for the teacher that he will learn what pure love of God, and His world, really means. From now on he is a *mumukshu* — a conscious seeker after liberation, a candidate for immortality — and has entered the path of Yoga. There we must leave him, with his quest and his teacher. Once found, let him never leave hold of him again, for God, through the teacher, will lead him over all the difficulties of the way to his goal.

X

SPIRITUAL INVESTIGATION

THIS TALK is to be about investigation and the stages through which an investigator generally passes before he or she becomes a pupil. Investigation has little to do with curiosity; in fact the two are opposed to each other. An enquiring mind is a blessing, but an inquisitive, curious mind is almost always a curse. To go off at full cry, like a hound after the quarry, may be an exhilarating *sport*, but a lot of energy will have been wasted if you find you have been on a false scent. Therefore investigation, unprejudiced enquiry, is an important quality for a true student — that is, one who does not run too easily!

In the classics of Adhyatma Yoga you will often find a list of qualities set out which are considered as essential if a candidate is to become intelligently attracted to this spiritual science, and investigation, or *vichara,* nearly always heads the list. Now the brand of investigation which is meant here is a special one. It is not an impulse to collect data, as the Jackdaw of Rheims collected the Cardinal's ring and other impedimenta. If one collects a mass of information about Yoga out of curiosity or acquisitiveness, one will become what our teacher used to describe as 'a sackful of books, animated by life'.

The kind of investigation which is prized by the teachers is produced from a mixture of qualities. The desire to grow (not so prevalent a desire as you might suppose), a belief in the existence and accessibility of knowledge, *and* a reverence for it: this mixture produces promising material — someone who is 'teachable' — perhaps the highest compliment Dr Shastri paid anyone. How he would scan the horizon for the approach of such a one, and how he valued and built on this quality of teachability when he found it!

Adhyatma Yoga runs the risk of being undervalued and called 'theoretical'. The West has a certain knowledge of Hatha Yoga, the physical Yoga, but this high and traditional Yoga is still in its pioneering stage in this country. Possibly this is because it has nothing occult or secret to teach and nothing to hide. From the outset, the goal of the Yoga, liberation of man's spirit from ignorance and from the bondage and dictation of his mind through the instrumentality of self-knowledge, is openly set out for the eye to see. But what the logical faculty sees is one thing, and what the higher power of the mind will reveal when it is awakened is another. Subtlety and purity of understanding is required in order to investigate and appreciate this Yoga, but this does not call for great intellectual attainments. It can be developed by a discipline and inner training, which was evolved long ago by great spiritual psychologists, and has been tested by time and results. It can be stated that if it is practised with continuity of purpose and in accordance with the traditional rules, it works! And it is available even today.

Although these seem to be trite and conventional words, the inner happenings they hint at by implication are far-reaching and astonishing to an unprejudiced investigator; and for this very reason the training must be carried out with moderation and patience. In one of the classics, there is a verse which says: 'This *Atman*' — *Atman* means the supreme Reality — 'This *Atman*, of which the high yogis speak, most subtle, beyond perception, must be realized step by step, and not by sudden violence'. Therefore it is desirable for both sides, the teacher and the candidate, to carry out investigations before entering on the training.

The investigations which a teacher carries out are traditional. Has he got someone before him whose secret desire is to become a sackful of books in order to astonish the world or his circle of friends, or has he got someone whose determination is to rise above book-learning and reach the state of direct experience? He soon finds out, and by means which may seem curious to us. He does not test the enquirer's intellectual capacity, his power to grasp the subtleties of the philosophy, but he turns his attention to the nature of his motives, and he assesses this by the willingness of the candidate to pay for what he is seeking. Financial payment is of course not in question — that would be too easy. It involves the offering up of precious energy, to be used in ways mystifying to the candidate, and the practice of patience, obedience, enthusiasm and other apparently homely virtues.

The candidate will also wish to investigate on his side, for he has got to be sure that he really wants the commodity offered and also that he is willing to pay the price demanded for it. Now, when one faces a work of art or of inspired thought, or a science, spiritual or otherwise, one is presumably unfitted at first to form a true and unprejudiced estimate of its value. One must therefore pay the subject the compliment of taking time to accustom oneself to its rarefied atmosphere, by keeping oneself open to change and the invasion of new ideas. This sounds dangerous, but provided the end in view has been defined and is not pseudo, it has its place and value. Reverence is also essential, not necessarily reverence for the particular art or system of thought one is facing, but reverence for the fact that perfection and beauty do exist, and that it is within the realm of possibility that they may reveal themselves here.

To develop this attitude and make it creative, it is necessary to seek out the sources from which the subject under investigation draws its strength. In other words, the candidate must turn to its classics. He will never be able to recognize and revere the grandeur and subtlety of this Yoga, for instance, if he persists in making a study of the works of 'Jagadguru Maha Mahatma Henry Robinson' — he will only discover, after very great difficulty, what 'Jagadguru Maha Mahatma Henry Robinson' hoped the Yoga would be. Therefore, for fruitful investigation he must go to the works of the great lights of the Yoga, to the philosopher Shri

Shankaracharya in his commentaries, or to the writings of such God-realized sages as Swami Rama Tirtha or Swami Mangalnath, or to the text-books of scholars such as Radhakrishnan and others. While poring over these classics he will unconsciously be absorbing the standard of perfection which is theirs, and he will eventually become immune to the second-rate. This sounds a very intellectual pursuit, but every shade of approach is offered by these great teachers. They paint the true background of the subject and give instruction suitable for all kinds and conditions of men.

After a preliminary and general study of their works, the candidate may feel that he can allow himself a little more licence, and he begins to investigate some apparent inconsistencies in the teachings. For instance, he will have read that the Yoga *invites* experiment and investigation, and now he learns from the classics that the fundamental nature of man, Consciousness Absolute, the supreme Reality, cannot be investigated or known by the mind, for Reality, being infinite, cannot be apprehended by a finite object, and the mind, being inert and composed of matter, can only have the effect of finitizing whatever it considers. If the enquirer has consciously preserved an attitude of reverence, or perhaps one should call it impartiality, he will wish to investigate this apparent discrepancy and will not necessarily think that he has discovered a flaw, long hidden and undetected, in the philosophy. He will therefore try to widen his mental horizon.

He will now find that whereas it is common knowledge today that below the conscious mind there lies a subconscious region, the repository of latent desires and emotions, a snake-pit of suppressed activity, it is not so well known, nor is it believed by all in the West, that there is a supra-conscious region also. Here is located (if one can use such a term) a high intuitive faculty. It lies behind and above the conscious mind of every individual, but it only becomes operative when the mind has been mastered and quietened by the practice of meditation. This power is the power of direct perception and spiritual intuition; through it, knowledge comes instantaneously and not through a conscious process. It forms the medium through which God or Truth touches and transforms the being of man, as one sees Him doing in the great fresco of Michelangelo.

Now the field of investigation is opening out to the enquirer, and what has he discovered?

The most important claim which has been made is that every man has infinite possibilities within himself — every man, and not only every saint — and that, given that he submits these qualities to cultivation and his ego to manipulation, these possibilities will become actualities, and he will emerge free and fearless and a source of liberation and joy to others. This claim has been substantiated many, many times. The teachers look on it as the normal course of events. For just as a living embryo must in due course be born and become manifest, so must each man inevitably experience the living Truth within him; but in the case of man, he can retard the time of his deliverance, and he suffers by doing so.

Now let us suppose that the investigator says: 'Well, this is a gigantic claim, so let us test it out. As I understand it, I am not going to be allowed to grow, for many of my qualities are going to be weeded out, and the faculties on which I lay such store, modified. Of all my powers, I most value my mind. Why this down on the mind? Why must it be virtually put out of action by segregating and controlling it? Why can't it be developed, so that it may become an asset and not a liability?' In other words, he is for half measures, hoping against hope that if he acquires a certain degree of control over his mind, he will be able to relax every now and then, go off duty so to say, and feed it with indigestible food by allowing it to watch television and see Snowball win the 2.15, or attend a performance of 'The Perfect Murder' at the cinema.

The answer to this question of the investigator is best given by altering the position, and imagining that the question is being asked about the sacrifices demanded from, say, a boxer during his training, or even from the jockey who is going to ride Snowball. The enquirer would then see at once that strict training is of course essential, and that a temporary restriction of worldly activities must be undergone if the goal is to be achieved. 'Ah yes', says the investigator, 'but the examples you have given deal with temporary training, not with a life pursuit such as Yoga. The worldly training soon comes to an end, and then the fruits can be enjoyed'.

Well, friends, we sincerely believe, and have been promised, that Yoga need not be a life pursuit. It was designed to be a temporary training, for its fruits are meant to be enjoyed in this life. When its aim has been achieved, it will become superfluous, for the man who reaches the goal of Yoga (and there are many who have done so) can do anything and live anywhere, for he is no longer confined as we are, but has become a universal man. This means that his prejudices *and* his preferences (a most important point this) have faded out before the direct light of his recognition of the unity of all phenomena and of their basic divinity.

In *World Within the Mind*, a part of the great work *Yoga Vasishtha*, which was translated by Dr Shastri, there is a description of such a man. It says: 'He adores and recognizes the supreme Spirit within himself, that Spirit which is self-effulgent, and which needs no illumination or incense to enhance it, the One before Whom all things are alike and equally good'.

Now the investigator makes his final enquiry, and if the answer is satisfactory, surely he will become a pupil. He still desires to know why, if all is passing, a thought or a desire, which must also be passing, should be held to have such infinite repercussions and be considered as capable of exerting such binding power. Now he is coming nearer to the crux of the matter, to an enquiry into that force, the mind, which can make or mar him, and he is now within the orbit of its attraction. But the fact that it cannot destroy him, as a candle flame can destroy a moth, is evidence that he has within himself a power superior to it.

We can only give an indication of the line of investigation the candidate must pursue in order to get the answer, for answer there is, to his question, although he will probably have to become a mature yogi before he appreciates it. That which is termed Reality, Truth, the Infinite Consciousness, forms the basis of all the phenomena, which it endows with spurious life and actuality. Matter, whether gross or subtle, provides on its side a medium of varying densities for the manifestation of Consciousness. Consciousness, as known by the yogis, is all-pervasive, unmoving and changeless in its nature. It is the medium of its manifestation — phenomena — which, being finite, cause it to appear to be broken up and active in character.

In the old teachings or illustrations in the classics, it is said that this divine substratum is sleeping in metals and rocks, half-awakened in animals and birds, awake in man and, it might be added, manifest in the God-realized man. But this is only another way of saying that it is the density of the medium of manifestation which causes the Consciousness to appear as sleeping, half-revealed or fully awakened.

Matter then, according to the Vedanta philosophy, provides a medium for the manifestation of Spirit, and it is energized by it, and this law also applies to man's instruments, for they are composed of subtle matter. Man has two sets of instruments, the outer and the inner. His outer instrument is his physical body, and his inner is the *antahkarana*, or the thinking, feeling, experiencing, emotion-producing principle, for which the only English word is the collective term 'mind'.

According to this teaching, consciousness is not a property of the mind. Mind is the vehicle for Consciousness. As was said, all matter, due to its proximity to Consciousness, is energized and in constant motion, and the subtle matter of which the mind is constituted, is no exception to this. The mental activity which we call thought, desire and emotional reaction, is termed a *vritti* in Sanskrit. A *vritti* is a wave in this subtle matter, which has a direction. It can be a simple recording of an impression, raising an instinctive reaction only, in which case it will have no aftermath, or it can be born from and coloured by imagination, memory or egoism, and it will then sink, as has already been described, into the subconscious region of the mind and become a subconscious mental activity.

It might be thought that when a mental wave has spent itself outwardly and subsided, it has dissipated, but this is not so. It has only become hidden, subtle and stored up, and it will manifest again when associations cause it to rise to the surface. The untrained man imagines that his actions and reactions, his thoughts and emotions, are worthy of serious consideration by himself and everyone else, because they are unprejudiced judgements with no past history; but he is wrong. They are often the result of hidden mental conditions, which may have existed, according to the philosophy, for incarnations. They have been drawn to the surface through the law of association, and they will, in their turn, create fresh *vrittis*, and these *vrittis* will produce another set of mental activities in due course, and so the wheel grinds on, and the feeling of imprisonment and frustration increases.

It is in this sense that the mind is considered such an unpredictable and dangerous possession. But how can its direction and control, which is so urgent, be done? The first means is to convince oneself through meditation that one is not the mind, but the independent owner, controller and architect of the mind. It is more possible to manipulate something with which you are not identified, and therefore great stress is laid during the training on detachment, which is the practice of *non-identification*, and on control, which teaches conscious *selection*, that is, selection of what the mind takes in, as well as what it gives out. These two qualities, non-identification and selection, make it possible for impressions to enter the mind uncoloured and undistorted by desire or emotion, thereby producing less food for the subconscious *vrittis*. Any practice which tends to increase the sense of mastery over the instruments is a valuable and vital practice, but the pupil cannot rest there. It is not sufficient to shut down the avenues of activity — there is no growth in that. The pupil must learn to inhabit the supra-conscious region of his mind, where being and quiescence, rather than doing and activity, is the law. Then he will be able to begin his positive, creative labours, and for this, meditation will be his tool.

I will now give you an illustration of the value placed by the teachers on this training of the mind. One day we were in the National Gallery with Dr Shastri. We were sitting at the end of one of those interminably long rooms, and he noticed a little child at the other end trailing along to join his mother, who was sitting near to us, holding a bun, well exposed, in her hand. The child was looking about him at the pictures as he made his way towards us, casting a professional eye over the picture of a dog or child, smiling to himself over a flower, increasing his pace when he came to pictures he didn't understand, but all the while coming to his real objective — his mother and the bun. Dr Shastri looked at him for a while and then said: 'There you see an exemplar of an intelligent, first-class pupil. He has a sense of direction, no confusing sense of possession, likes or dislikes, but detachment, the enjoyment of a spectator and the purpose of a pilgrim'. I expect Dr Shastri meant that the child did not stand motionless before one picture and say, 'I could look at this for ever!', nor did he rush past one he didn't like and keep looking back, saying, 'How horrible, how horrible!' He enjoyed, experienced or discarded, and then passed on.

Well, there it is, and the investigator will hardly recognize himself now, walking along the interminably long Gallery of the world, enjoying its sights, yet passing on towards something he has now glimpsed and longs for.

Friends, this talk is done, and if, notwithstanding what was said at the beginning about Yoga not being theoretical, you still find it so, the fault is mine. For this Yoga is not a skeleton with its bony structure intact and in place; it is a living thing and will infuse those who come near enough with its life. Whatever people may say, it will be suitable for the West when it has been studied and understood. Our teacher knew and loved many God-realized men in India, and in nearly every case they were active people who had followed some profession until their highest duty became clear — to mingle with the people of the world and pass on the Truth to them.

Our teacher's own teacher was a householder who worked on the railway; Swami Rama Tirtha, about whom Dr Shastri has written the book *Scientist and Mahatma*, had been a university professor; Pundit Baijnath was an eminent and practising barrister, who never gave up his profession; and Shri Nirbhayanandaji had been an inspector of schools. All these were illumined beings and the very fact that these great men sent our teacher to this country and placed such great hopes in him is proof positive to us, his pupils, that this country is capable of receiving the Yoga he brought with him.

XI

CONSTRUCTIVE LIVING

According to Adhyatma Yoga — the Yoga of Self-knowledge — life is to be lived consciously and according to plan, and has as its object the yoking or joining of the individual soul to the supreme Spirit, through enlightened action. The word 'Yoga' means a yoke in the sense of 'that which joins' and the word 'Adhyatma' is defined by the great philosopher Shankaracharya as 'that which first shows itself as the innermost self or soul in the body and which turns out in the end to be identical with the supreme Reality — God'.

There are many paths and Yogas, but the hallmark of true Yoga is that it is spiritual in character, and teaches the way of approach, or rather of return, to God. No true Yoga has anything to do with the acquisition of psychic powers or with the occult.

There is more than one way by which a man can return to his source. Some take the way of knowledge, some of devotion and others, the path of action, and there are Yogas dealing with each of these paths. Adhyatma Yoga is a synthesis of all three. According to its teachings, the pupil must perform study, devotion and service concurrently, and it is as important for him to become proficient in the practical side as it is for him to master the philosophy and the art of meditation.

Adhyatma Yoga is a spiritual science and it claims to reveal to man the power within himself whereby he can purify and control his mind and then transcend its limitations, finally obtaining union with the supreme Spirit — not after death, but during his life on earth. This divine power has its seat in the higher will or intuitive faculty (*buddhi*). Its existence is not recognized until the lower mind has been to some degree purified and stilled.

Wise performance of action is essential — not clever, but wise performance. The 'inner equilibrium' which is stressed in the *Gita* implies co-ordination of body, mind and spirit — the right relationship between the Spirit and its instruments. This balance is the secret of constructive living and it can only be attained when the pupil has learnt to live *in* his body and mind, and not *as* his body and mind. This state is brought about by a method which involves purification, meditation, devotion and service of mankind, that is, inner preparation and outer practice.

It is the accepted opinion in the West that the beliefs held by Eastern peoples lead to escapism, lethargy and fatalism, that whenever a crisis occurs they start to pray and cease to act. If this is so, the fault does not lie with the teachings embodied in their scriptures. You will constantly hear: 'Oh well, if their beliefs are so wonderful, why are the people in India...?' I am sure if we were asked by an Indian why the West abounds in insurance companies, since Christ said: 'Take no thought for the morrow', we should feel very misunderstood and rule out the question as irrelevant!

The fact is, that hidden in all the great scriptures of the world lie those truths and methods which could deliver man from his bondage, if they were not almost forgotten. Everyone wants freedom and happiness — freedom from fear, from the domination of the mind and the emotions — but as with everything else, spiritual or material, there is the price to pay and so the desired state remains unattained.

Every science has a technique, but it is only successful when its practice is based on the interior knowledge that produces it. So it is with the spiritual science. The quality of the outer life is determined by the quality of the inner state from which it springs. Action is the measuring rod with which we can assess the depth and reality of our spiritual convictions. No matter what we may affirm in our meditations, the acid test is how to meet the everyday happenings.

Those who know, testify that successful meditation is dependent on the quality of the life lived during the twenty-four hours, and certainly, no life can be constructive or progressive which is not fed and based upon meditation and communion with God.

It is in the tradition of Adhyatma Yoga that whatever the pupil receives, in the form of knowledge or spiritual power and enlightenment, shall be offered back by him to his fellow men. The true yogi is a worker among men and a participator in life. Should he wish to live a life of contemplation, he is only allowed to do so after he has lived in the world for a very long time. This rule is based on the psychological fact that there are very few hearts and minds which can remain at their best if kept on one line without a break for a long time. The palate ceases to savour the same taste after a time; the digestive organs lose their power if presented with the same food, day in, day out; so the heart and mind lose resilience if kept on one line of action without interruption, be that line inner or outer. The monasteries of old were centres of industry as well as centres of prayer. Sheep farming, wine distilling, missal illuminating, writing, teaching and nursing — all these activities were carried out in addition to the spiritual activities.

Therefore, in order to live constructively, man must bring the same qualities to bear on his actions as he brings to bear on his meditations and prayers. What are these? *Alertness:* he must be awake to the significance of what he is doing. *Concentration:* his mind must be one-pointed in performance. *Devotion:* he must offer whatever action he performs to the Lord. *Dependence:* he must depend for his light and strength on a force greater than his own.

These qualities are not to be had for the asking. They are, like everything else, subject to cultivation. Discipline is the way to cultivate them. Discipline is not coercion, but the acceptance and following of certain rules, laid down by the wise, out of their own experience. An undisciplined man can do nothing lasting, inwardly or outwardly. He is constantly getting in his own way and is a danger to himself and to others. In a *Sufi* mystic classic, it is said: 'Through discipline, heaven has been filled with light; through discipline, the angels became immaculate and holy'.

What are some of the preliminary rules laid down by the great teachers to guide their pupils in the way of constructive living? One of the most important is that the pupil shall concentrate his power on his own duty and on no-one else's. St François de Sales says that God requires the faithful fulfilment of the merest trifle given to us to do, rather than the most ardent aspiration towards things to which we are not called. The pupil is required to fight where he stands and not to try and change his circumstances into others which he considers would be more propitious. He performs the duty brought to him by his *karma*, but he performs that duty as an offering to the Lord, and so makes it a fertile opportunity to learn the spiritual lessons of detachment, patience, equanimity and so forth.

Next in importance is complete harmlessness in thought, word and action. Thought is put first because mental acts are much more powerful than physical ones. Complete harmlessness is based on the acceptance of the spiritual law of the universality of consciousness — that there is one Spirit pervading the whole creation, that the universe is one, and that consequently, all that live in it are of one family. The Yoga teaches that man is a part of the great whole and not an independent unit, that he is connected and interconnected with every atom, that what he does, does not affect himself alone, but has a universal significance.

Another prerequisite is active enquiry, based on an urgent desire for knowledge, which leads the enquirer to seek out those who know and endows him with the willingness to learn from them. To know does not mean to know theoretically, but to experience; it does not lead to conviction, but to certainty; it does not mean to define, but to divine. In the *Mathnawi* it is written:

> Endeavour to find out the commands of God from one who is united with God. Not every heart understands the commands of God. Either you must have the touchstone within your own soul, or, if you know not the Way, do not go forward alone. Without need, Almighty God does not give anything to anybody; therefore quickly augment thy need, O Needy One, that the sea of His bounty may surge up in loving kindness.

Harmlessness, a sense of urgency to know, then the patient cultivation of reverence and devotion. Reverence is the 'Open Sesame!' to any door. The true artist, scientist and saint all reverence the object of their search, and as reverence increases, egoity decreases. Devotion can grow out of reverence. You may have every ingredient to hand necessary for a good meal, but if fire is absent, it is useless and no meal can be cooked. Similarly a man may be eager to know and to conform to the discipline, but without reverence and some instinct for devotion, he lies becalmed.

It is for the aspirant to yield the fruits of the experience and knowledge that he gains to anyone in need of them. In order to give, one must have a surplus out of which to give. 'No burdened one shall bear another's burdens.' Surely the criticism so often levelled against spiritual training, namely that it is selfish and egotistical, is the reverse of true. Spiritual wealth must be amassed like any other wealth and should be freely given when acquired. A bankrupt cannot be a giver.

These are some aspects of the inner discipline by which a man may become master of himself and cease to be a slave of circumstance.

The mind is like a sponge: if you put it in milk, it will absorb milk; if in vinegar, vinegar. If you interest the mind in gross things, it will bring forth crudity and grossness. If you immerse it in God, it will mirror the thought of God. It is a very delicate instrument, and a moment of anger, greed or fear, tears its fabric. For the mind to discover the spiritual truth, it must live in devotion, for it is not only creative, but imitative. It takes on the quality of whatever it identifies itself with, in the same way that the crystal assumes the colour of the object near it. But the mind must be purified and stilled if it is to reflect the pure light of God. If you wish to hasten this process, seek out one who has purified his mind, and learn the spiritual science from him. As St Thomas à Kempis says: 'Enquire willingly and hear in silence the words of holy men'.

Now although the inner way of controlling the mind is a science in itself, there are some simple hints which can be given here, which may prove useful. You cannot control anything unless you stand apart from it; in the same way, you cannot control the mind as long as you identify yourself with it. Force and repression will do no good: if you use repression, you are tacitly acknowledging the strength and reality of the thing you are trying to disregard, and it is not disarmed but only kept in check. Therefore, instead of attempting to repress the mind, one must learn to control it by realizing the significance and truth of the spiritual teachings, by recognizing what the mind is and treating it accordingly. If you acquire the habit of witnessing the mind, you will observe that it delights in chain thinking. You will find that it loses its lightness by loading itself with desires, fears and false imaginings, and runs continually from one thing to another. In *The Crest Jewel of Discrimination*, a well-known Eastern classic, it is said:

> If the mind strays ever so slightly from the ideal, it becomes externalized and bounces like a ball, inadvertently dropped on a flight of steps.

Chain thinking is as vicious as chain smoking and can only be cured by giving the mind a worthy focus, and keeping it constantly employed. We have said that the mind is like a sponge and should be immersed in beauty and in those things which will bring it a wider knowledge and range, such as poetry, music, literature and, if you are fortunate enough to possess an alert mind, philosophy. Everyone may experience difficulty in making these efforts at first, due largely to want of alertness and torpidity of will, but there are many simple exercises for training the will, as, for example, resolving to use the left hand for two hours daily. You will be surprised how many excellent reasons you will find for giving it up, after a few moments. Another exercise is to set oneself to read a passage, or to keep the mind concentrated on a particular subject for a specified time which, however short, is rigidly adhered to. There are many other exercises of this kind, apparently childish but of great value.

These are the ways, according to the teachings of Adhyatma Yoga, that the constructive life, progressing towards liberation, is to be lived. To this state the Yoga is leading the pupil, to a life of balanced recklessness, lived for man and to the glory of God.

XII

KNOWLEDGE OF THE SELF

I HAVE been asked to provide some information about the status of knowledge and learning in the East in the hope that this may be of some use to readers of that valuable and ancient work called *Direct Experience of Reality* attributed to the great philosopher Shri Shankaracharya, which our teacher, Dr Hari Prasad Shastri, has recently translated with a commentary.

At the present time, India is in the process of westernizing herself, so far as the activities of the various departments of learning are concerned. As a result, floods of books giving technical information and analyzing, tabulating and assessing the value of the various subjects are pouring from her. But this does not affect the importance, or the position, she has always accorded to knowledge since the ancient times, when the daring conceptions of Advaita Vedanta, the philosophy of non-duality, were first conceived, and it is to be hoped that this position will never be disturbed.

Now you may be thinking: 'What is this? We imagined that we were to consider knowledge and learning, and we are already talking about one department of it only, philosophy, the philosophy of non-duality, a separate and surely a self-supporting branch of knowledge'. Well, this is the first and most important difference between the Eastern and Western conception of knowledge. To the Westerner there are many departments of knowledge, each quite separate from the other, having different origins and different goals, and it is held that provided a man who wishes to study one of them has persistence, intelligence and an accumulation of facts, information and figures at his disposal, he will probably be successful, and end by 'knowing his subject', as they say.

In the East, however, knowledge has always meant the knowledge of Truth, the supreme Knowledge, to which I suppose we in the West must give the name of philosophy, although there is a difference. For in the East, this philosophy, or spiritual science, was regarded as a way of *life*, not merely as a way of *thought*, as it is here. Knowledge was originally envisaged in the East as a spiritual unity, from which the various branches of learning sprang and drew their strength, and often an interpretation of their findings as well.

This science of the Self or Truth was first given forth, by inference, in the *Vedas*, the most ancient scriptures of India, and as the old sages saw little difference between the goal of wisdom and that of the different branches of learning, they sheltered and supported all learning. The various branches of learning, in their turn, paid tribute to the scriptures, regarding them as the root from which they collectively sprang. When the modern Indian scientist, Sir Jagadish Chandra Bhose, made his researches into the sensitivity of plants and metals, he gave the credit for what he discovered to the *Vedas*, for he said that the facts he had been able to establish had already been foreshadowed there, and this had influenced him to make his experiments.

In the *Chandogya Upanishad*, there is a story on this point, where it is shown that the highest Truth is guarded in the ancient scriptures. It tells how one Narada once approached a teacher and said: 'Please teach me, Sir'. The teacher said: 'Tell me what you know and afterwards I will tell you what is beyond'. Thereupon, Narada recited a long list of different subjects he had studied: the four *Vedas*, ethics, astronomy, medicine and so on *ad infinitum*. But he then confesses that he still does not know the supreme Truth, the Self, and says: 'I have heard from men like you, Sir, that he who knows the Self overcomes grief. I am in grief. Do, Sir, help me over this grief of mine'. Then the teacher consoles him and he assures him that the Truth he seeks does in fact lie hidden in the *Vedas*, and that he will now reveal and teach it to him, and Shri Shankaracharya in his commentary on this instruction, says:

> If a royal procession approaches, then, though we do not see the King because he is hidden by flags and umbrellas, you will say: 'There is the King', and though we cannot point him out, we can say at least that he is different from all that is seen. The Self is hidden in the *Vedas*, as the King is hidden in a royal procession.

The various branches of learning, astronomy and so on, were called in the olden times the 'lower knowledge', while the spiritual knowledge of the Self was called 'the higher, or superior, knowledge'. This higher knowledge, then, is that knowledge where the goal is complete freedom: freedom from the limitations naturally imposed by the mind and circumstances. It is gained through *training*, mainly training of the *mind*, which persists until that mind knows or reveals its true stature and powers, and also its ability to apprehend and inhabit *three* worlds, not *two* only, namely the physical and mental worlds *and* the supra-mental world, the world of Spirit.

The ancient thinkers of the East recognized and paid tribute to the supra-mental, as well as to the normal powers of the mind. They tested the scope of these higher powers — inspiration, intuition, mystical experience and the like — and satisfied themselves, not only that they were reliable when traditionally produced and manipulated, but that they could be used in the subsidiary branches of learning as well.

In the West, on the other hand, knowledge was, and still is, expected to produce more and more information about the physical world in which man's body moves, and the mental sphere in which his mind moves. In all branches of learning, information has to be checked and counter-checked by the empirical mind itself, and the data must stand up to experiment and not rely on experience. Experience, they say, can tell you anything you wish to hear, and is therefore counted out as a reliable guide.

But the West is not yet fully acquainted with the traditional training called Yoga which, in the East, has to be undergone before experience and not imagination — and pseudo-imagination at that — can come into operation and solve problems unanswerable by the mind in its normal condition.

Now this fundamental difference of status has influenced the findings of the various departments of learning in both East and West. But having indicated this fact for your further study, if you are interested, we plead guilty to the charge of over-simplification, and pass on from the general to the particular.

In the East, where knowledge is, or was, considered to be a unity, all branches suffered if the spiritual science went temporarily into eclipse; whereas in the West, the great departments of learning were a law unto themselves, and continued to attract many, irrespective of whether the spiritual health of the people was good or not. It is true that this was not always the case, for at certain times there has been a close relationship between the Church and learning. In the Middle Ages many of the great institutions of learning, such as existed in France at the time of Charlemagne, and some of our own colleges and schools also, were founded by the Church or were intimately connected with it. But these institutions were not so affected by the fluctuations caused by academic differences over doctrine and procedure, as were the branches of learning in the East when there was a dearth of illumined teachers to give out and interpret a changeless Truth.

Now the book *Direct Experience of Reality* was written at just such a time in India. The spiritual knowledge had been temporarily withdrawn and all other branches of learning were suffering accordingly. When Shri Shankaracharya was born in the eighth century AD, there was a lack of spiritual teachers, great heresies abounded and the spiritual science was being put to materialistic ends. Philosophical bickering was going on all over the country, and this great and illumined sage spent his thirty-three years of life in re-establishing the law of *dharma*, or righteousness, and then the system of traditional training, which alone would restore the great secrets of the higher knowledge to the people. He turned to the established scriptures and gave forth commentary after commentary upon their teachings, which are still unsurpassed. Then, in order that the work should be cherished and expanded and further expounded according to tradition, he founded four great monasteries to the north, south, east and west of India, where even today the abbots are called by his name — Shri Shankaracharya. When he died, the old conception of the sacred nature of all learning and its basic connection with the spiritual truth had again been firmly established, and the great disciples who had surrounded and learnt from him during his life, carried on the work of re-interpreting and commenting on the ancient writings, and the works of their teacher and these commentaries are still available and used today.

You will have noticed that it was said that Shri Shankara first re-established the law of *dharma*, or righteousness. It may seem strange that he did not give precedence to the purity of the spiritual beliefs and the significance of the ceremonial, rather than exhort men to turn to universal goodwill, compassion and service. But although his commentary on the *Bhagavad Gita*, for instance, is full of philosophical teaching and argument, the instruction which stands out as especially directed and given with a universal purpose, is his exhortation that the pupil shall practise self-sacrifice, universal compassion, devotion and egoless service. He held that it was only by living these qualities that the mind would be pacified and expanded, and that when also strengthened by the yogic training, it would then be ready for the recognition of the supreme Knowledge or Truth — the Truth of the nature of the Self. In other words, until the mind had been made subtle and pure through discipline, and the pupil had carried out in practice the implications of the belief, his mind would neither be freed, nor would it be able to comprehend the living Truth underlying the philosophy.

One of the methods employed by Shri Shankaracharya to resuscitate the inner truth is revealed in his treatment of the practices of Hatha Yoga, the physical Yoga of postures, *pranayama* and exercises for the production of power, so popular in the West today, and apparently equally popular in his lifetime also.

In *Direct Experience of Reality*, he deals with this. For instance, in Hatha Yoga some pupils aim at maintaining complete silence over long periods, only communicating with the outer world by writing their messages on a slate, quite oblivious of the fact that the amount of mental energy involved in both processes is the same. He says about this:

> Who can describe Brahman or God, from which all words turn away? Even this world is beyond the range of words. This then is the real silence of the

> wise, known as the natural or the inner silence; the silence of the lips is only for the dull-witted. (108/9)

This natural inner silence of the heart or mind arising from contemplation, was interpreted by the Hatha yogis as the refraining from actual speech for the purpose of conserving energy.

Then as to posture he says:

> The inner state which permits the uninterrupted contemplation of Brahman is to be considered as the best posture — this is the real posture and not those which merely disturb one's ease. The mere straightening of the limbs like the branches of a withered tree, is not equilibrium. (112, 115)

There are well over one hundred postures known in Hatha Yoga and anyone who has seen photographs of some of them will be able to understand what Shri Shankara means by saying that they merely disturb one's ease and confuse the issue. In each case Shri Shankara goes back to the inner and original reason for these outer practices and shows the loss of spiritual insight which caused them to become so complicated and also so important. He shows that by posture was originally meant an inner uninterrupted state of alert and yet relaxed attention, capable of being maintained as long as the contemplation itself lasts:

> Make thy vision the vision of illumination and see the world as *Brahman*. This is the supreme vision and not to look at the tip of the nose. (116)

Shri Shankara says more than once that a controlled mind, fortified by meditation and enquiry into the holy philosophy, will accomplish naturally what all these practices attempt to do by unnatural means, and much more. He has a good deal to say on the subject of breath control or *pranayama*, and here again he urges that the mind shall be controlled by devotion and meditation and not by reliance on violent methods. It is all set out in *Direct Experience of Reality* so that anyone who is interested can study it for themselves.

Having got thus far in this attempt to say a little about knowledge and learning, I wonder whether it is at all clear why the Eastern knowledge or wisdom was possessed of such an inspiring and vital power that Shri Shankara and his disciples gave their lives to save it from eclipse. The knowledge bestowed on his followers by Shri Shankaracharya is the Truth given in the philosophy of *Advaita,* or non-duality. It is hidden in the *Vedas*, it is postulated in certain of the *Upanishads* and other treatises and in the works of the great teachers, and it is affirmed through the inspired utterances of the seers who *saw* the fact of this Truth directly. Finally, it has been demonstrated in practice by its followers, not only by flashes of illumined understanding but through reason and logic as well.

The truth which this knowledge reveals is that God or *Brahman* is the only Reality and that therefore man and *Brahman* are identical. Every book written by our own teacher Dr Shastri had this truth as its basis, although in some cases he was engaged in clearing and making walkable the path by which newcomers to this thought might approach it.

The sentence 'Man is identical with *Brahman*' argues that his powers are infinite, though potential, and that he will have to become free and experience his divinity directly, before he can rest and know the bliss which lies at the root of his nature; and that even where his empirical mind is concerned, its powers are generally untapped by him, and will only emerge as a result of training and discipline.

What kind of person can aspire to study this knowledge of the Self? Anyone! Shri Shankara says that anyone who suffers is eligible to embrace this philosophy — anybody, that is, who feels dissatisfaction with his present spiritual state and is willing to exert himself to prove to himself that release and freedom are facts.

Then why aren't we all God-realized? We still believe in the existence, and feel the attraction, of what we can see and experience through the mind and the five senses, and we say to ourselves that, for the present, we cannot afford the time or the energy to experiment on that which we cannot see.

I will just indicate a few points about this ancient and traditional spiritual training, without which it is held that the deeper significance of the philosophy cannot be known.

Before ever training begins, both sides must satisfy themselves on certain points. The pupil must satisfy himself that this knowledge and what it is said to bring, and the training which will bring it, is what he wants. Of course, he cannot have a full understanding of its significance at the outset, but he *can* get a very good idea, through enquiry, through reading and association with those who are already under instruction in Yoga.

The teacher on his side has got to satisfy himself that the pupil's powers of co-operation, determination, as also his need, are sufficient to carry him over the difficulties and apparent restrictions and obstacles which will meet and accompany him for who knows how far on his way. The teacher often evades the pupil at first, disregarding his requests for instruction, and when he does at last accept him, he used, in the old days at any rate, to employ him as a servant, to cook and clean, and fetch and carry for an indefinite period.

Now many will say: 'Oh well! That is obviously done to humiliate him and get rid of his ego'; but it has a far deeper purpose than that. For it reveals, not only to the teacher but to the would-be pupil himself, the depth and intensity of his determination to get what he wants. In other words, it helps him to identify himself with his purpose. Many find to their surprise that they do possess this fixity of purpose, once it has been brought to the surface to confront obstacles. When he was a young man, the composer Haydn was kept back in his study of music, not only by the want of money, of which he had none, but also through ignorance of the laws of musical composition. He therefore took a position as a valet to a certain conductor and composer, Signor Porpora, merely in order that he might find out what he needed to know about counterpoint and so on, quite oblivious of the fact that this was not one of the qualities expected of a valet and that he had none of the qualifications of an ideal man-servant. But this didn't deter him, and he did not leave his victim until he had rifled his mind of the information he needed, after which he was able to forge ahead.

All through the training, the eye of the teacher is on the growth of comprehension and will in his pupil, rather than on his ability and keenness to carry out the usual practices of Yoga, though these are of course very important and will become increasingly so. The Truth can be analyzed and thought over from the first, and it is this which brings the ripeness which the teacher is watching for. Dr Shastri once said: 'The realization of the identity of man's individual spirit with the supreme Spirit is the apex of the teachings of the Advaita, but it is not to be attained merely by hearing and accepting it. It needs deep thought, careful analysis and the guidance of reliable authorities as well. If, even after deep thought and analysis, this identity is not realized, then the process must be repeated again and again, until such knowledge *is* acquired'. It is of no use to exclaim: 'All is *Brahman*', or 'All is *maya* — illusion', when you have not been through these preliminary stages. It is only a pain and an outrage to all who hear you. Such people are called *vacha jnanis*, which means 'Those who are liberated by word of mouth or speech only'.

Therefore the preliminary testing of the pupil by the teacher also gives the pupil time and opportunity for thought and investigation on the significance of what he is about to subscribe to. Take one instance alone: the importance he will have to give to righteousness or *dharma*. Some people, and nearly every pupil at first, find it hard to credit that an intellectual system of thought, as the *Advaita* seems to be, should place such importance on what they look upon as merely an ethical principle. But if the enquirer has truly grasped even a hint of the implications of the identity of Consciousness, which is a tenet of the philosophy, he will of necessity have to place importance on a universal outlook and on the conception of the brotherhood of man, and he will begin to realize that the impulse to harm another, let us say, is tantamount to an impulse to harm himself, and that the qualities of sacrifice and service are not moral obligations but natural reactions.

Now this attitude will only be able to be maintained when an inner certainty about the basic position has been attained. So you will see that the practices of mind control, meditation, contemplation and repetition of the *mantram*, can only assume their real importance when the mind which executes them is beginning to expand beyond its personal territory and its personal desires for fame and power. This is why training will never succeed, in this Yoga at any rate, where the pupil does not give reality and pay allegiance to the beliefs on which it is based.

XIII

THE MOTIVE POWER IN YOGA

SO FAR we have tried to give a very general idea of Adhyatma Yoga, and I do wish that we could know what sort of a picture we have succeeded in painting before you. It might be depressing, but it would certainly teach us a lot about our shortcomings. Have we, I wonder, given you the idea that Yoga is pre-eminently a way of life, and not a way of training, a pure and righteous way of life it may be, but nevertheless one which will last as long as the yogi lasts, and will teach him how to get more satisfaction out of this mortal existence than his fellow men and women can get? Or have we made you think that Yoga is the Eastern name for a scientific and psychological method, at once ancient and new, which will prepare the mind for fresh discoveries and give it wider scope and empirical interests than fall to the lot of an ordinary untrained man? Both pictures would be misleading, and for two reasons.

Firstly, Yoga is not a cause which produces desirable results. It is the effect of a hidden cause — a compelling cause — the slow but inevitable revealing in man of the presence of the basic power of the supreme Truth, the power which, in the end, and *through* the practices of Yoga, will be found to be identical with his real Self.

Secondly, Yoga is not a way of life, it is a way of training, and as such it must have its climax, just as every other training has a climax. A man should enter Yoga for one purpose only, and it is that he shall pass out of it during this life as a liberated being. For the climax of Yoga is no other than the awakening of the disciple to his true nature which, as we have said, is divine, transcendent and identical with the non-dual spirit of Consciousness, Existence and Bliss Absolute.

These words do not belong to the vocabulary of Yoga. They form the backbone of the philosophy of Advaita Vedanta, for they are its considered and final affirmations. The function of the Yoga is to hand on certain accredited methods through which the physical, mental and subtle equipment of the learner may be rendered fit, first to test these affirmations, then to grasp their significance, and finally to accept them, not intellectually and theoretically, but as the result of direct experience and recognition.

There is but one power manifesting in varying degrees in both the macrocosm and the microcosm and it is the power of *Chit* (Consciousness Absolute, or God) and there is a certain resemblance between its manifestations in nature and its manifestations in man. For example, both have their winter, their spring and their summer. But in the case of man, his seasons do not recur; they appear but once, and his autumn will provide but one harvest only, after gathering which he will go out no more. In nature, the warm rain, the appearance of flower and leaf, announce the approach of another spring. They are the visible effects of oscillations produced by this divine Consciousness which, though massed and motionless in itself, yet, in a mysterious sense, when clothed in the magic of *maya* or duality, forms the background and incentive for variety, for visible beauty and for quality.

But in man, the indications of growth which appear before his spring, or rather before his awakening, are different. In him the inner rhythm is symbolized by unfoldment, not by recurrence, and by the slow changing of his mental reactions and perceptions from darkness to Light. In the cosmos, the drama is played out again and again in cycles, at due times and seasons; in man it leads to the climax of his final liberation, and not to another seed time, the preparation for a future spring.

Still, the likeness between the manifestation of growth in nature and in man is not entirely fanciful, although it may seem to be so. For instance, that moment when the primal power, in order to manifest outwardly and consciously, turns in its deep hiding place within the earth, or within man's mind: that moment is known to both, and it is called the turn of the year. For months, the dark earth feels no movement and hears no sound, and for incarnations, man also, unconscious and instinctive, has been sensible of no inner activity. He has experienced joy and sorrow, it is true, but only instinctively; he has gained and lost with a bewildered feeling of frustration, but also with a sense of inevitability. To the untrained view he is like the winter landscape, no sign of growth anywhere. Then, at a given moment, his year turns and, like the earth, he begins to experience the consciousness of growth; that is, he awakens to a dim self-consciousness and a sense of direction, and he starts to explore, to enjoy and to suffer, consciously.

He is testing life as he knows it, and is

perhaps finding that it is giving way in his hands. But although not fully awake as yet, he is maturing his hidden qualities against the time when they will become essential to his progress. At last, during some blustery incarnation, the first real sign of his spring appears, for he, following a sense of direction which he has fashioned in himself while still in the dark, underground, comes to a Centre of spiritual learning and training, and offers his loyalty and his service in exchange for the knowledge he will receive there.

We know that the spring in nature is luxuriant and lovely. What beauties will man's spring have to show, now that it is approaching? Ah! my friends, this luxuriance, this wealth of sound and colour that we see around us in nature, is not the primary melody at the root of all things. It is but an arabesque, a descant! It is left to man alone to refine and train his senses sufficiently to catch and sing the rare and pure root-melody of the supreme Spirit, and to hear the soundless sound from which it springs. To do this, he will have to forsake manifold variety which excites, and come to recognize the limitless nature of the One, as against the appearance of richness of the many.

In this philosophy of Advaita, unity and universality are synonymous terms. The supreme Truth is held to be a unity, which expresses itself only in a consciousness of that unity. It is not to be apprehended by a mind given over to preferences and prejudices, in other words, by a mind given over to diversity. In fact it cannot be fully cognized by the empirical mind at all. Its presence can at first only be surmised, and then only when that mind has reached a certain degree of purity. The fact that the supreme Self *is*, will be revealed to man in the first instance through its effects in *maya* and not through its own nature in himself.

As has been said, in the world of names and forms, every object, mental and physical, is infused by the supreme Spirit, and only appears in manifestation by virtue of the unseen presence and proximity of that Spirit. These objects reflect its power in varying degrees, and the drama of existence lies in the process by which the sense of perception of the viewer is gradually refined so that all objects are seen to mirror forth the subject more and more completely, until at last their essence stands revealed as identical with it.

Man is a world in himself but, like the empirical world, he also, as an object, is infused by this divine essence; but here again, the fact is hidden from him and from others at first. The Self first reveals itself to him in the form of a remembrance and a recognition. Like recognizes like, and the Self recognizes the Self. This recognition takes place in the apex of his mind, known as the higher *buddhi*, the ground of inspiration and the higher supra-mental faculties. This higher *buddhi* only becomes active when the lower mind has become passive; but if the pupil believes this, and works for this end, the somewhat dry practices of mind control will take on a new and creative character.

According to the Vedanta, the composite instrument through which man acts, experiences and perceives, and through which he will finally make the discovery of his identity with the supreme Spirit, is called in Sanskrit the *antah-karana* or inner organ. This inner organ, or the mind, is held to consist of five aspects or functions — *manas*: the lower mind, or the unselective recording function; *chitta*: the function of emotion, will and memory; the lower *buddhi*: the function of empirical reason, the logical and discriminative faculty; the higher *buddhi*: the home of the intuitive, inspirational quality, and which does not manifest itself until the uncontrolled lower mental activity has abated; and *ahankara*: the ego, the villain of the piece, which is not only the power behind the throne but is often found firmly seated upon it.

In company with all other phenomena, the *ahankara* is dual by nature, being an admixture of the sense of self-reference and fixation and a reflection of the supreme light of Truth. There is a resemblance between the mind in the body and the moon in the sky. Both shine with a borrowed light, the moon reflecting the light of the source of all empirical light, the sun, and the mind reflecting the rays of the light of supreme Consciousness.

During the night — that is, during the period of empirical ignorance, while the positive and direct light is still hidden — both moon and mind will furnish the best, in fact the only, aid to the faculty of vision. But they both give borrowed light, only man does not know it. It is dim and uncertain, but yet he is not aware of this, for he has not yet envisaged the source of their shining — in one case the great Sun, in the other the supreme Truth. Therefore any suggestion that his mind could be superseded as a luminary, fills him with alarm. It is only when the brilliant Sun of Truth has mounted in his sky, and rules his mind, that man awakens to the true meaning of the word *light*.

Now we know what happens to the objective moon when the sun rises. It does not need to be put out of action; it puts itself out of action by extinguishing its candle light in the ocean of light which is that victorious Sun, and henceforward it hangs like a pale disc in the sky, a reminder of things past. Just such an abdication is performed by the mortal mind when the full light of divine knowledge dawns. It ceases to be the sole source of vision, for its findings are blurred when compared with the certainty established by the light of Reality. It can therefore no longer be regarded as the true and only source of knowledge, although it is still employed by its owner on the more menial tasks.

I hope that I have shown that Self-revelation and the eclipse of ignorance and egoism — in other words the rising of the non-dual Sun of Truth, and the waning of the moon of duality — are the motive powers behind this Yoga.

Most of the practices given to the disciple during his training fall into one or the other of these two categories — those furthering the rise of the positive and supreme knowledge of Self, and those which bring about the breaking down of the power of the ego. The positive practices are those which promote a constant remembrance of the nature of the Self which is described in the dictum *Kham Brahman* — All is *Brahman*, and *So 'ham* — I am He, or *Om*, the mystic syllable denoting *Brahman*. These practices are the practice of meditation and the repetition of the *mantram*, and in both the focus for contemplation is the basic truth of the *fact* of the supreme Reality or God. The result of their long and dedicated performance is that the mind slowly loses its restlessness and pre-occupation with detail, and allows the presence of the great supra-mental powers of inspiration and the sense of freedom and universality to reveal themselves within it.

It must always be remembered, however, that the practice of meditation does not cease when you rise from the posture, when you 'break your meditation', as it is called. The sense of the meditation should continue in an interior form as a background for the activities throughout the day, or at any rate it should be resuscitated and contemplated at intervals during the day.

The repetition of the *mantram* is a practice which is based on laws of sound and rhythm which are not generally known in the West as yet. These *mantrams* have power, and are only imparted at the discretion of a teacher, but the rhythm established by a reiteration of the idea or the sentence, and the actual sound of it, affect and change the inner rhythm of the pupil and serve to intensify the vision of Self which is growing up, perhaps unperceived, in his mind.

The result of these two practices, which should be a growing recognition of the reality of the omnipresent and supreme Truth, will not take place if their practice is restricted to the actual time allotted to them. The disciple must train himself to make the Truth contained in the meditation a background to his life, his day and all his activities, and not merely an intermittent interest.

When the words 'a background to his life' and so on are used, don't imagine that this involves active and uninterrupted thought on the subject throughout the day, for this would obviously be impossible in a busy life. It involves a preliminary recognition of the root of all meditations: the all-pervadingness of the divine Power and then firm reliance on this fact. *Brahman* must be visualized as all-pervading and as being as essential to man as the air he breathes and on which he depends for life. The fact of the universal yet invisible presence of air, and one's dependence on it, is a certainty established at the back of every mind, and all activities are carried on under the assumption that it is a fact. This assumption is the fruit of an original and an instinctive acceptance, and it does not need to be supported by a constant mental effort.

In the same way, the Truth, or the fact of *Kham Brahman* — All is *Brahman* — which has already been consciously accepted during meditation, should be relied upon and not merely thought about during the day; that is, it should be visualized as the all-pervading element which forms the background for all action, and which provides the power and the knowledge through which action may be successfully carried out.

The practices which bring about the waning of the power of the ego are, first and foremost, worship or devotion, through which the disciple learns to forget his own self and to live intensely and selflessly in the aura of another focus. Worship should be able to obliterate the sense of ego, but often it gives rise to a more subtle form of it, born of a false sense of uniqueness, and a proprietary interest in the object of worship. However, the risk must be run, for there is no practice which attacks the ego so directly as devotion and worship.

Many will tell you that they cannot concentrate their hearts on an *Avatara* or a saint or a teacher, or on a symbol of God such as *Om*. They call this duality, and say that they prefer to 'contemplate non-duality' — which you will see, if you are not involved in the matter yourself, is a nonsense. You will also see that devotion calls for a certain recognition of, and reverence for, the state of perfection manifested by the object of worship, and that this successfully puts the one who is worshipping completely out of focus. Therefore let us merely say at present that worship is a very necessary, glorious and traditional part of yogic training.

The last practice is mind control and the directing and conserving of its energies. Here again it must be repeated that none of these practices will take root and become natural, that is, become a part of life, unless they are played out against a background of spiritual awareness. If practised by themselves, they may appear to have results, but these results will only be temporary, because the mind always goes where it finds, or expects to find, most joy, and unless it is trained to long for the direct sight of the divine Truth, mind control is only control by force and no more, and its results will disappear if the control is withdrawn.

There is a poem by an old poet of the last century which describes the passing nature of these gestures compelled by an outer force only. It can be used to illustrate what I have been saying, although the poet certainly never meant his poem to be thought of in this connection. He says:

> I drew towards me a bough of May
> That I might see and smell.
> It bore it, in a sort of way,
> It bore it very well.
> But when I let it backward sway,
> O it were hard to tell
> With what a toss, with what a swing,
> The lovely thing,
> Resumed its proper level,
> And sent me to the devil.

After that the poet goes on with his own affairs, which are not strictly relevant to our theme.

You draw the mind towards you and think that by bringing it under direct scrutiny you are controlling it, or rather that it is willing to be controlled. But you are wrong, for it is only submitting temporarily to a superior force and it will put all that right when your concentration wavers. With a joyous bound it will resume its proper level and send you to the devil.

The only force which can control the mind is that superior force which can make it control itself, the force of a growing longing for something it is beginning to desire, greater expansion and joy through direct knowledge of the truth contained in the meditation. If that remembrance is forever being laid aside in favour of more immediate interests, the longing and the love will not spring up to direct the mind, and mind control will be a name only.

Now of course, this is the ideal progress of an ideal disciple, but it is possible for it to be carried out either in whole or in part during a life of action. How this is done has already been described in earlier chapters, and the possibility of such a life should again be stressed now for we must practise it in part even from the start.

To go back over the points for a moment. The motive power behind Yoga is the supreme Reality slowly manifesting itself within the heart of the disciple and so awakening in him the longing for its climax, Self-realization. This longing is produced by keeping the Truth at the back of the mind throughout the working day and relying on its presence as we rely on the air we breathe, and bringing it forward at intervals, or at given times, in order to intensify the certainty of its presence and its truth. Where this progression in training is followed even in part, the application of force becomes out of place, for the mind will, in the end, control itself through its intense desire to see and know.

As a refreshment and to end with, here is a short passage from the *Maitri Upanishad* which shows with what unbroken purpose and patience the search for God must be conducted by the disciple and what glory and freedom awaits him at the end of the journey. It is written in symbolic language, but I think it is understandable. The 'shrines' mentioned are probably the bodily, mental and subtle states passed through by the disciple during his search:

> OM. He enters slowly into the Hall of *Brahman* as a miner seeking minerals enters a mine. Then through the instruction of his teacher, he breaks through the shrines, which consist of food, breath, mind and knowledge, and reaches the last shrine, that of blessedness and identity with *Brahman*. Thenceforward, pure, tranquil, imperishable, firm and independent, he stands in his own greatness,

and having seen the Self, he looks on the world of birth and death as one alighted from a chariot looks on its revolving wheels. OM. (VI.28)

XIV

THE EVER-EXPANDING VIEW

THIS TITLE has been chosen because it gives a promise of growth and surprise. Any situation which is fully revealed from the beginning has no challenge. Many believe that the revealed function of life is to afford a field of experiment for science, and that the facts about the origin, meaning and goal of life will, in the end, surrender to experiment and application. Such people, the devotees of reason and certainty, often find themselves unaccountably depressed and repressed.

Most people are looking for cures, not cures for the basic cause of their uneasiness and frustration, but cures for the effects of that cause. Sleepless nights, fear, indigestion, heart trouble, giddiness — well, we won't go on! They seem to feel that if these troubles could be corrected, preferably not through the usual channel — the skill of a doctor — there would be a chance of life becoming liveable again. Now if they were to say: 'I want to clear the decks before I sail out on a voyage of discovery, so kindly give me exercises to cure my indigestion and depression', we might chafe, but still, their reason for wanting their pain cured would have something vital in it, namely that they might afterwards be able to sail out to sea unfettered, say, by a grumbling appendix. But it never works out like that. So the situation is evidently beyond our puny control and calls for enlightened action, action by those guardians of the distressed, the great teachers of all ages and all faiths, to whom this state of things is the inevitable outcome of unharmonious and artificial living and thinking.

Our own teacher's Guru, Shri Dada, used to say that it was no use trying to teach something to a starving man, that first you must feed him, and then teach him. This is particularly true today. Television, the press and others who think they know, are trying to nourish man on synthetic food, and yet at the same time they keep on assuring him that he is 'fed up', if you will forgive the horrid expression. Man is not fed up. He has no food inside him at all — no food, that is, which has any nourishment in it — but he has a hunger so deep that he has almost ceased to feel it. All the same, until this hunger *is* satisfied, he will not be able to take an intelligent interest in the Vedanta theory of perception, or the concept of *Maya*, or even in politics or sociology. This hunger of his is a basic necessity, for he must be satisfied that there *is* something worth living for, that in fact there exists a world of experience about which he knows nothing as yet, but which he will be capable of entering and conquering some day. That is what he wants to be sure of.

When George Mallory was asked why he wanted to climb Everest, he replied, 'Because it is there!' Unless we *know* that something *is* there to conquer, any preparations we make for an ascent will be rather in the nature of those military exercises which are designed to keep a man fit, in case he should be needed one day.

There are two traditional methods of teaching in the East. The first, inaugurated by the great philosopher and teacher, Shri Shankaracharya, and followed by his disciples, reveals the goal at once. Having fired the imagination of the pupil and sown in him a determination to reach the top of the mountain, it gives him the method of training and discipline which will enable him to arrive there. The other method, followed by the true Hatha yogis and other schools, trains the body and mind first and then, if it is traditionally practised, the goal is revealed to the pupil.

Adhyatma Yoga belongs to the first category, the school of the great Shri Shankaracharya.

It seems, therefore, that the first task before us is to convince our fellow men that there *is* something there, so to say, something which is supremely desirable and, furthermore, that they are capable of reaching it. When I say 'our fellow men', I mean the average man, not the scientist, who is a devotee of Truth already, nor the artist, who must be a dedicated disciple of beauty in any case — but people like many of us, who have little specialized knowledge and no scientific data to go on, but who have the qualities of an explorer hidden within them and who therefore have a right to the guidance of those who have reached the peak of existence and have seen what they describe; or better still, have become what they describe.

The mind appears to be so constituted that it will not relinquish its hold on anything until it is presented with something else more attractive. Furthermore, it has a peculiar capacity for protecting itself which, speaking very broadly, is rather like the capacity of the blood to coagulate when an injury has been done to the body. For the mind can form protective habits when confronted by threatened change. But a habit can be the pupil's friend and not only his foe. If he can, from the beginning, cajole the mind into forming the habit of *vichara*, or unprejudiced enquiry, this will first help him to enter the new world, and then it will sustain him when he experiences the doubts and revulsions which nearly always visit the one who is weighing up the *pros* and *cons* of a matter in which he may get involved.

By this time an intelligent reader must be thinking: 'Well, I can see no difference between this method of approach to knowledge and the scientific approach. The mind is catered for in both cases, surely.' Our teacher used to say that the mind is such a deceiver and a rogue that any method of circumventing it is permissible. Man has always been dependent on the mind, for it has apparently been shaping his destiny for incarnations and has now become a dictator, unwilling to share its power with any.

Now, if as a result of the preliminary practice of *vichara*, or unprejudiced enquiry, man should decide to study this Yoga, he is beginning to interest himself in a science which will ultimately bring about the abdication of the mind — not its extinction, but first its abdication from its supreme position of dictatorship, and then the installation of another and higher power in its place. This higher power at present lies hidden and will not reveal itself until the mortal mind has been controlled and stilled.

But the mortal mind will surely never countenance such a project. Why should it? Well, when the mind awakens to the position, it doesn't, and it proceeds to give a lot of trouble, marshalling a host of preconceived notions around it to protect itself..

I believe that when a drug addict is under treatment, the dose is slowly lessened, but not completely cut off from the beginning. Just so, the one who is experimenting in this science does not immediately cut his mind off from its normal activities. But he does try, all the while, to manoeuvre it into such a position that it will begin to lose its assurance, born of years of undisputed power, and become lit, or at any rate made lighter, by proximity to the living flame of the Truth of Advaita.

The quickest way to create this change in the mind is to place it in the proximity of those who know, and who therefore have nothing to gain or to lose. When I use the word 'proximity', I do not necessarily mean physical association with a teacher — not yet. Dr Shastri used to tell his audiences that they must first decide to become pupils, and then they could look for a teacher. To place oneself in the proximity of Truth can mean reading and brooding on the living words of those teachers who have seen and become the Truth, and who have left inspired utterances to guide others. At this stage such a course is probably as instructive as contact with their living minds would be.

The first move therefore is enquiry, but enquiry of a special kind. This enquiry has two stages. The first stage is the receiving of the Truth, which is being heard or read, without question or criticism, and the acceptance of it as something which is being given to the hearer personally, and which it is vital that he should know. The second stage involves going over this instruction again in slow motion, so to say, subjecting it to a more specialized enquiry. This means assessing its universal as well as its particular significance, and thinking over its practical aspect also. Constructive criticism has its place here, and many may think it is making its appearance rather late in the day, for why should the Truth or any other knowledge be received at first without criticism? The answer is that this is recommended in order to break down one of those protective habits of the mind which we spoke of, the habit of preconceived ideas, a habit which robs everything of its freshness and impact and is the bulwark of caution and so-called 'balance'.

There is another and deeper reason why the critical powers of the mind should be kept in abeyance during the first stages of *vichara*. The transfer of a thought involves also the transfer of a ray of the power or state of consciousness of that mind which once conceived it, which is why the great spiritual documents take the form of assertions and not reasoned arguments. This transference cannot be carried out if the mind is full of its own reactions — its native likes and dislikes, its 'boisterous weather'. So if the habit of premature criticism is allowed to intrude and dictate, we shall not gaze on the ever-expanding view, or, if we do get a glimpse of it, we shall not have the grace to admit that it presents anything we have not seen before.

Those who refuse to have their attention arrested by anything which is new to them, who are armed *cap à pie* against a complete acceptance of anything, what to say of enthusiasm for anything — we all know them, and we know that this danger is probably lurking in ourselves as well. It *is* a danger, for if such people continue the search at all, while still preserving their often hidden reservations, they will become at best *vacha jnanis*, those whose knowledge is confined to words and superficial understanding only.

Once I went to hear a great pianist and I sat beside an old couple. I was rather interested in them, because they did not look as if they were going to get much from the music and I wondered why they were there. But I noticed that as a certain work began, they became completely concentrated. It was brilliant and technical and at the end they relaxed, smiled at each other and whispered: 'Millie can play it faster'.

Well, no doubt Millie could play it faster, for Millie was merely skidding over the surface of the work. She was a musical *vacha jnani*, one with superficial aptitude, who had recognized one quality in the work only and was battening on that. No, friends! Mere repetition is always dead. True knowledge cannot pass unless it is sent out from a living centre. The words of an enlightened man are still charged with his creative power, although he may have lived centuries ago, for at one point in his life, he threw down his protective weapons and lit the flame of the recognition of Truth within himself, and so awakened the higher sense which manifests as inspiration, intuition and instantaneous perception, and which rises in the flame like a salamander, while the mortal mind surrenders its limited powers before it.

You will probably think that this is an extravagant claim and that it is most certainly put forward in extravagant language. We do not think so. We see it as a statement of fact, but it is one of the reasons why the pupil has to accept discipline and training, for his instrument, the higher mind, or *buddhi*, must be refined if it is to become aware of such subtle intimations of spiritual power and, in the end, be able to pass that power on to others.

It is not too much to say that there are very few people who are not suited to practise some aspect of Yoga. The teachers were and still are psychologists, and they suit their teachings to the minds of their pupils. They can bring them to the peak of life by many routes; by the path of devotion, or of service, or by the path of knowledge. But in every case they first arrest their pupils' inner attention by revealing the goal to them; that is, they first give their pupils a sight of the thing that is there and which is going to make their efforts worthwhile.

What is this thing that is there — the goal not only of Yoga, but of existence, a realization of which will awaken the inner life and the joy of that life, for which man has thirsted for so long? We can only repeat in essence the words of our teacher on this. This priceless Truth, the thing which is there, the giver of bliss and fearlessness and freedom, is the identity of the supreme Reality, the One-without-a-second, with the Spirit, the 'I' of man. This identity is timeless, yet it is recognizable by man at any point in time. This Truth reveals in effect that man is omniscient and that he can know the Truth about his nature during his life here on earth, and in fact must know it, if he is to be fulfilled and at peace. This is the half-forgotten knowledge which makes him restless and dissatisfied until he has re-discovered and brought it to the surface and made it his own again.

Like tributaries of a mighty river, subsidiary truths spring from this central fact: the truth of the brotherhood of all living things; the power of this knowledge to banish fear and restriction, and to reveal the magnitude and responsibility of the individual, who is, in fact, one with the whole; and also the revelation of the paramount importance of meditation and contemplation which form the bridge, so to say, between the mind's two powers, the mental and the supra-mental, leading the traveller to the vantage point where he can recognize the authority and truth contained in the traditional formulae: *Kham Brahman* — All is *Brahman* or Reality — and *So 'ham* — I am That.

This is immemorial wisdom and it is inviolable, not able to be used until the seeker has, through the traditional training, become so purified that he realizes its significance in his being and is henceforth incapable of doing harm to himself or to any other thing. This knowledge will not become his until the poison of his egoity has been extracted from him, nor will he have the right to use it until he has become universal in outlook.

In other words, unlike the followers of modern schools of mind control, who are told that they will become supremely attractive, and successful in business, if they obey certain rules, the seeker will not be able to bend this knowledge to his personal ends, nor will he wish to do so. But from the moment that he bows in reverence before the vast concept of the Advaita, he will become conscious that he is of royal origin and must one day assume complete control over his people, that is, over his senses, his mind and much more. Once he has taken up this position of independence, his self-respect is restored, the view is expanding, and his desire is quickening.

Well, this is 'the Thing which is *there*', which will make life worth while. But we must now go back to the ascent which leads to it. I propose to spend the rest of this talk in trying to give you an idea of the stature of two great yogis of this school who reached this summit of being, and then I will give the names of books which can help both those who know nothing as yet about this Yoga and those who have already done some study on the subject.

The name of the first yogi I have chosen is Shri Swami Vidyaranya. I have chosen him because he will answer the question which is so often asked: 'Can I live in the world and engage in a profession and still practise Yoga?' Well, he did it, magnificently. He lived in the fourteenth century and was highly trained in all branches of secular learning; that is to say, in mathematics, rhetoric and so on, and quite early in his life he was accepted by a spiritual teacher.

During his youth the Mohammedan invasion

of India was in progress and her spiritual heritage was in jeopardy. It was a time which called for determined resistance and this was organized and inspired by Vidyaranya. As chief adviser of the local ruler, he raised an army and defeated the Mohammedans in the south of India and formed a new empire. He supervised the building of its beautiful capital and also countless temples and universities.

All this time he was a servant of his Guru, and was a disciple worthy of the name; but by the age of fifty, he realized that although he had reached the summit of worldly ambitions, he was still a learner of the spiritual science. So he then decided to renounce his worldly honours and wealth, and he became a monk in the holy Order of Shri Shankaracharya.

From then on, until he died at the age of ninety, his activity found an outlet in the mental world and a great flow of philosophical works came from him. Among them is one called *Panchadashi*, or The Book of Fifteen Chapters, which is essential reading for any serious student of Advaita Vedanta, and has been translated by Dr Shastri and published by Shanti Sadan. His life showed a fair division of activity between the two worlds, and his value as a teacher is as high today as it was when he was living.

The other yogi I have chosen is connected with our Centre through our teacher. His name was Pundit Baijnath. He was a God-realized man and a barrister at the same time. He was born in the middle of the last century and was gifted with one of the prerequisites to true success in law, an analytical yet unprejudiced approach to learning. He studied law and, as he grew up, he became a very successful and sought-after barrister. But he had not yet met with his teacher, nor had he studied the spiritual science, although he felt the necessity for a Guru deep in his heart.

At last, one day, he met the great teacher, Swami Nirbhayanandaji, unexpectedly, in a garden, and very soon he had entered on his spiritual training. He used to say that at first he was made a captive by the brilliant intellect of his Guru, but that later on, he became aware that certain changes were taking place within him and he realized that these were due to the transfer of living spiritual power from his teacher to himself.

He never gave up his practice in the Courts, though he reached the highest state of illumination. He became a teacher himself and a protector of the poor and those who desired knowledge.

I chose these two men to try to show that Yoga and active life can be practised together, that is, if the pupil will plan his life to this end. The culmination of Yoga is the revelation of the true nature of man, but Yoga can help him at all levels.

Now about the living words of such great yogis. There are two categories of such words. The first category comprises *awakening* words, words which will not reveal their meaning at once, but which will give an indication of the inner presence of Truth, as you hear the sea booming and dashing against the rocks long before you come into its presence. These books have to be read and re-read and their quality absorbed by the inner sense, although they will also have to be accepted by the reasoning mind later on. The other kind of reading is the *informative* reading, the reading about training and the traditional tenets of the philosophy. Alternation between the two categories is the ideal activity, and I will give you the names of two or three books taken at random from each category.

In the awakening category there are the

Ashtavakra Gita and the *Avadhut Gita*, both translated by our teacher, and any good translation of the principal *Upanishads*, say the one by Radhakrishnan. In the category for immediate and useful information come Dr Shastri's *Teachings from the Bhagavad Gita* and his translation, with a commentary, of a work with a most difficult-sounding title but a very informative interior, *Aparokshanubhuti*, which, being interpreted, means *Direct Experience of Reality*; and also *The Crest Jewel of Discrimination**.

If you should decide to read any of these books, which would be a good preliminary practice, you will find that they give you a sense of the grandeur of the conception of Advaita and therefore of the necessity for a preliminary training and discipline, if you make up your mind to study it seriously; but I wish you good fortune in any case.

* A translation of this work with the commentary of Hari Prasad Shastri will shortly be published by Shanti Sadan.

GLOSSARY

Adhyatma the supreme Self.

Adhyatma Yoga the Yoga of Self-Knowledge; the spiritual science concerned with the real nature of man.

Advaita ['not two'] non-duality. The philosophy of Advaita holds that *Brahman* alone exists without a second.

Ahankara the ego; the 'I' taken as doer and experiencer.

Ananda bliss.

Antahkarana the 'inner organ' or mind of the individual; the thinking and feeling principle in the human personality.

Atman the higher Self of man, which is identical with the supreme Reality, *Brahman*.

Avatara an Incarnation of God; a direct descent of God to earth in a physical body.

Bhagavad Gita the 'Song of the Lord' — a spiritual classic in which the *Avatara* Lord Krishna summarizes the teachings of Yoga for his disciple Arjuna.

Brahman the absolute Reality; the highest Godhead beyond attributes.

Buddhi the faculty of intellect and intuition.

Chit Consciousness.

Chitta the faculty of memory and imagination.

Dharma the principle of order and harmony in the world; the universal law of righteousness; man's spiritual and moral duty.

Gita Song; a shortened form of *Bhagavad Gita*.

Guna wave-like principle or mode which pervades the whole of creation. There are three *gunas*, namely *sattva* (harmony), *rajas* (activity) and *tamas* (inertia).

Guru traditional spiritual teacher.

Jiva the individual soul.

Jivan-mukta one liberated-in-life.

Karma action and its consequences, determined by the law of cause and effect.

Manana reflection on the Truth which has already been heard.

Manas the lower mind.

Mantram a traditional prayer or invocation which is repeated with a rosary.

Maya the creative power of the Lord, by means of which the phenomenal world has been brought into existence; cosmic nescience, the veiling power which hides the reality of the Self and gives rise to the belief that the manifested world is real.

Nididhyasana uninterrupted and one-pointed contemplation of the Truth which has been heard and reflected upon.

Nirvikalpa free from mental imaginings.

Om a sacred syllable, given in the *Vedas* as the highest name of God; a symbol of the highest Reality in its various aspects.

Rajas the *guna* of activity and passion-struggle.

Samadhi unbroken meditation; a high state of consciousness in which the mind transcends the normal subject-object relationship.

Sansara empirical existence; the wheel of birth and death; transmigration.

Sat existence.

Sat-Chit-Ananda existence-consciousness-bliss, triple designation of *Brahman*.

Sattva the *guna* of harmony, equilibrium and light.

Shravana listening to the spiritual Truth.

Tamas the *guna* of inertia and darkness.

Upanishads ancient scriptures which give the essential yogic wisdom in philosophical form.

Vasanas tendencies or urges in the mind, due to latent past impressions and unfulfilled desires (*sanskaras*).

Vedanta the system of philosophy based on the *Upanishads*.

Vichara philosophical enquiry into spiritual truth.

Viveka spiritual discrimination between the real and the unreal.

Vritti a mode of the mind.

Yoga 'union': the science of the union of man with God; the technique and discipline by means of which the individual soul can achieve conscious union with the supreme Spirit.

INDEX

INDEX

NOTES

NOTES

SHANTI SADAN PUBLICATIONS

by Marjorie Waterhouse

Training the Mind through Yoga

The Power Behind the Mind

by Hari Prasad Shastri (original works)

The Heart of the Eastern Mystical Teaching

Meditation — Its Theory and Practice

Wisdom from the East   Echoes of Japan

The Search for a Guru

etc.

by Hari Prasad Shastri (translations)

Ashtavakra Gita   Avadhut Gita

Direct Experience of Reality

Teachings from the Bhagavad Gita

Panchadashi   World Within the Mind

Ramayana of Valmiki (3 volumes)

etc.

For book catalogue and details of current public lectures held at Shanti Sadan and elsewhere, contact:

SHANTI SADAN Centre of Adhyatma Yoga
29 Chepstow Villas, London W11 3DR
Tel. 0171 727 7846 Fax. 0171 792 9817